THE PHILOSOPHY OF BODY

The Philosophy of Body

Edited by
Michael Proudfoot

Blackwell Publishing

First published as a special issue of *RATIO*, 2002

350 Main Street, Malden, MA 02148–5018, USA
108 Cowley Road, Oxford OX4 1JF, UK
550 Swanston Street, Carlton South, Melbourne, Victoria 3053, Australia
Kurfürstendamm 57, 10707 Berlin, Germany

First published 2003 by Blackwell Publishers Ltd

Library of Congress Cataloguing-in-Publication Data has been applied for

ISBN 1–40510–895–9

A catalogue record for this title is available from the British Library.

Set by Cambrian Typesetters Ltd.

For further information on
Blackwell Publishing visit our website:
www.blackwellpublishing.com

CONTENTS

INTRODUCTION

Since Descartes, much has been written about the Mind/Body problem – about what the connection is between minds and bodies. But philosophers have overwhelmingly concentrated on one side of the alleged divide, and have studied "the philosophy of mind" in great detail. Much less has been heard about "the philosophy of body", and, when bodies *are* discussed in connection with the Mind/Body problem, then it is usually only one part of the body, the brain, that is mentioned.

The neglect of the body starts much further back than with Descartes. There has been, as Nietzsche observed in *The Genealogy of Morals*, a general Western devaluation of the body in favour of the mind. The view has been that the life of the philosopher should be dominated by reason, rather than the emotions. Nietzsche diagnoses the Western philosophical tradition as a form of asceticism that ignores all that is untidily and even disgustingly connected with the body and its demands. Plato in the *Phaedo*, has Socrates agreeing that the true philosopher despises the pleasures of the body, and would be best off without a body at all.

This devaluation of the body has meant that "the philosophy of body" does not bring to mind a particular set of philosophical problems, in the way that, for example, "the philosophy of mind" might. But it is easy enough to see some of the questions that the philosophy of body might include. What are the philosophical consequences of human beings' embodiedness? What role does the body play in our experience of the world? What effect has the sort of body we have make to our experience of the world and of other people, and to their experience of us?

But there have been increasing signs of interest within Anglophone philosophy in the body in the last ten years or so, and it is likely that this interest will increase much more rapidly over the next decade. There have been several contributing causes of this interest. The first arises from the great interest in the last 50 years or so in questions of personal identity and self-identity. A second cause arises from the interest in what distinguishes human beings from computers. A third cause has been the continuing rapprochement between so-called analytic and continental philosophy. In continental philosophy, specially within the work of the phenomenologists and in Merleau-Ponty in particular, there has been a concern with embodiedness, from which analytic philosophers are gradually realising they may have something to learn. A fourth cause has been the development of feminist philosophy within the last 50 years, in which embodiedness, to begin with especially sex and gender, but later much more generally, has played a central, indeed, defining, role.

This collection of newly written articles reflects all of these causes and includes a wide variety of treatments of the subject. This volume, like the others in the series, had its origins in the Ratio Annual Conference in Reading in April 2001 on the Philosophy of Body. That conference, at which Hubert Dreyfus, Sean Dorrance Kelly, Quassim Cassam and Alison Adam were the speakers, was primarily aimed at philosophers working within the Anglophone analytic tradition, with the goal of discovering what might be learnt from the work of philosophers who have worked, or drawn upon, the phenomenological tradition, and, in particular, from the work of Merleau-Ponty. The 2001 Ratio Conference was thus continuing the theme of some previous Ratio conferences ("Arguing with Derrida", for example, in 1999) of the ways in which the analytic tradition can learn from philosophical work in other traditions, and the discovery that there is an actual fact a convergence of interests which may have been masked by the more entrenched attitudes of the last few decades.

Quassim Cassam and Max de Gaynesford work in the mainly analytic tradition of Kant and Peter Strawson. But their work is informed by an understanding of the phenomenological approach, and by a consideration of problems that arise in both analytic and philosophy and in phenomenology. In Cassam's article in this volume, he takes issue with Sartre and Merleau-Ponty, and argues that the idea that one's body is a thing among other things is a coherent idea. He further argues that awareness of one's own body is a necessary presupposition for having the concepts of primary qualities and hence objective experience.

De Gaynesford, in his article, argues that the sort of bodily awareness that is involved in perception may be sufficient for introspective self-awareness, without having to bring in the idea of agency. The phenomenological movement in the twentieth century gives a central importance to bodily experience in our exploration and understanding of the world and our selves. De Gaynesford's conclusion might be thought to be at odds with this position. But his argument is close to Merleau-Ponty's claim that there are two distinct ways of understanding the position of an object when we see it. The first way is essentially cognitive, and the second way is essentially bodily, which Merleau-Ponty calls "motor-intentional". Sean Kelly, in his article, defends Merleau-Ponty's claim. Kelly argues that in the second, motor-intentional, understanding of the position of an object, the distinction normally made between the content of the attitude of an intentional state does not apply.

Hubert Dreyfus's article continues this theme, through a discussion of the work of Samuel Todes. Todes was an American philosopher who died in 1994 whose work deserves to be far better known. In his book *Body and World* Todes contributes to the debate within analytic philosophy about non-conceptual intentional content by drawing on Gestalt Psychology and on phenomenology, and, once again, Merleau-Ponty in particular. Dreyfus shows how Todes too, distinguishes two modes of perception. The first is a practical mode of perception which arises from our unified body acting in the world to meet our needs. The second arises when we withhold our activity, and our practical perception is transformed into a detached perception of the qualities of an object, experienced independently of the object. It is to be hoped that Dreyfus's paper will encourage an interest in Todes and his contribution to this contemporary debate.

Alison Adams and Iris Young both consider feminist challenges to influential contemporary ways of thinking. Adam discusses AI from a feminist position, and argues that AI has generally ignored those bodily ways of knowing that phenomenology emphasised. In particular, she argues that the development of embodied robots has crucially ignored feminine aspects of embodiment. In addition, AI, and more recently A-Life, Artificial Life, have left very little room for such important human characteristics as passion, love and emotion.

Iris Young discusses recent feminist challenges to the concept of gender. Some writers, such as Toril Moi, have argued that the concept should be jettisoned, because it depends on false distinctions. It should be replaced, Moi has argued, with the phenomenological concept of the lived body. Young is sympathetic to

Moi's suggestion, but argues that the concept of gender cannot so easily be discarded, for it still has an important role in understanding structural processes and inequalities in society.

The final article is by Michael Brearley. Brearley is the former England cricket captain, as becomes evident in his article in the relation of one of his dreams. He was a professional philosopher before he became a professional cricketer, and is now a practising psychotherapist. Brearley illuminates our understanding of the body and the mind by presenting a psychoanalytical model of the mind. In this model our conception of the mind emerges from a more primordial body-mind nexus, to which, under pressure, we might sometimes regress. Brearley's final words serve fittingly as a conclusion to the book. "Human bodies cannot be reduced to mere collections of chemicals. Mind permeates our bodies, and vice versa."

I would like to thank those who presented papers at the 2001 Conference, as well as Max de Gaynesford, Iris Young and Michael Brearley, who kindly agreed to provide written contributions. Support for the conference was received from the Analysis Trust (in the form of bursaries to enable graduate students to attend), the *Mind* Association, and the Forum for European Philosophy, to all of whom thanks are therefore due. I would also like to thank Javier Kalhat Pocicovich thanked for his editorial assistance with this book, and to give special thanks to Jean Britland of the Reading Philosophy Department for her invaluable assistance in the organisation of the conference.

Michael Proudfoot
Department of Philosophy
University of Reading
RG6 6AA

1

REPRESENTING BODIES

Quassim Cassam

I

In his *Essay*, Locke proposes that what makes something a 'body' is its possession of primary qualities. What Locke describes in this context as a 'body', we might prefer to describe as a 'material object'. In Locke's sense of 'body', mountains and suitcases are bodies. Sounds, holograms and shadows are not. The qualities which Locke identifies as primary are solidity, extension, figure, motion or rest, and number. Of these, solidity is said to be the most important or fundamental primary quality, the one that is 'most intimately connected with and essential to Body' (1975: 123). .

Given that what makes an object a material object is its possession of primary qualities, it is plausible that in order to think of an object as a material object one must think of it as something with primary qualities. Since one cannot think of something as a possessor or bearer of primary qualities unless one has concepts of primary qualities, it would be worth giving some thought to the conditions under which it is possible for one to acquire and grap such concepts. I want to examine the thesis that awareness of one's own body is a necessary condition for the acquisition and possession of concepts of primary qualities. I will call this thesis the *bodily awareness thesis,* or BAT for short. If, as I believe, BAT is along the right lines, then we should conclude that awareness of one's own body is a necessary condition for thinking of objects as material.

To think of an object as a material object is not just to think of it as a bearer of primary qualities. It is also to think of it as one among many such things. The question which this raises is whether one can think of one's own body as an object in this sense. At one point, Merleau-Ponty characterizes one's own body as a 'sensible sentient' (1968: 137), as something which sees and touches as well as something which can be seen and touched. A familiar claim is that that which sees and touches cannot properly be thought of as a 'thing among other things' (Sartre 1989: 304). If this claim is correct, there would be an important sense in which one cannot think of one's own body as an object and therefore as a material object. I will be arguing that this conclusion is mistaken. The most that can be concluded from the fact that one's own body is a sensible sentient is that one cannot think of it as what might be called a 'mere' body. My claim will be that thinking of one's own body as a material object among material objects need not be a matter of thinking of it as a 'mere' body.

II

Before going any further, more needs to be said about Locke's account of primary qualities. The plausible thought which underpins this account is that our most basic notion of a material object is that of a bounded, three-dimensional space-filler. To fill a region of space is to exclude other bodies from that region of space. For Locke, solidity is the most fundamental of the primary qualities because it is in virtue of their solidity that material objects fill space. In the words of the *Essay*, the solidity of a body consists in an 'utter Exclusion of other Bodies out of the space it possesses' (1975: 125). Figure and extension can be seen as primary qualities of bodies that are consequential upon their solidity.

Is Locke right to regard solidity as the primary quality which is most intimately connected with and essential to the body? In his *Metaphysical Foundations of Natural Science* Kant argues that 'matter fills a space only by moving force', that is, 'by such a force as resists the penetration, i.e. the approach, of another matter' (1985: 499). To suppose that the property of matter by which it fills a space is solidity is to suppose that matter fills its space 'by its mere existence' (1985: 497). In contrast, Kant's proposal is that 'only when I attribute to that which occupies a space a force to repel every external movable thing that approaches it, do I understand how a contradiction is involved when the space which a thing occupies is penetrated by another thing of the same kind' (1985: 498).[1] Thus, the moving force by which matter fills a space is repulsive force. Impenetrability is 'given immediately with the concept of matter' (1985: 509), and the impenetrability of matter

---

[1] See Warren 2001 for an illuminating discussion of Kant's proposal.

is a consequence of its repulsive force. Since material objects are composed of matter, and repulsive force belongs to 'the essence of matter' (1985: 511), an important part of what it is to be a material object is to be something which exerts repulsive force.

Is this a claim which Locke would dispute? Although force is not one of Locke's primary qualities, it is worth remembering that Locke connects solidity with impenetrability and that he represents the impenetrability of bodies as consisting in their possession of what Kant would call repulsive force. On the other hand, Locke's considered view is that the impenetrability of bodies is a consequence of their solidity.[2] To be more precise, Locke's idea is that impenetrability is a power and that solidity is the categorical ground of this power. This is what Kant rejects. He regards repulsive force as a fundamental force which cannot be further explicated. In particular, it cannot be explicated by reference to what Locke calls solidity. For Kant, Lockean solidity is an occult quality which cannot intelligibly be regarded as the categorical ground of impenetrability.[3]

In the present context, it is not important to decide whether Kant is right to be so dismissive of the proposal that solidity is the ground of impenetrability. What is important is the idea that part of what it is to be a material object is to exert some degree of force. Repulsive force is, however, not the only force which material objects exert. It is also plausible that for something to be a material object is for 'changes in its states of motion to be explicable by the mechanical forces acting upon it, and for changes in its motion to exert such forces' (Peacocke 1993: 170). On this mechanistic conception of force bodies have force insofar as they are in motion. In contrast, Kant thinks of repulsion as a 'dynamical' rather than as a mechanical force. In the words of one recent commentator, dynamical forces such as repulsion and attraction are ones which bodies have 'independent of their states of motion or rest' (Warren 2001: 111). The fact remains, however, that if primary qualities are the intrinsic or fundamental properties of material objects as such, then force, whether mechanical or dynamical, is a primary quality. By the same token, to think of an object as a material object is to think of it as something which exerts, and is subject to, the appropriate forces.[4] This is the basic

---

[2] See Locke 1975: 123.
[3] For more on this aspect of Kant's thinking, see Warren 2001: 103–6.
[4] For a closely related suggestion, see Peacocke 1993.

insight which I wish to extract from my discussion of Locke and
Kant.

What is the bearing of this insight on BAT? If force is a primary
quality, then one cannot think of an object as material unless one
has the concept of force. How, then, is the concept of force
acquired? It is in connection with this question that an argument
for BAT begins to emerge. The first thing to notice is that there
is, as Peacocke remarks, 'such a thing as the sensation of force. It
is experienced when, for instance, a heavy book is resting on your
lap and pressing downwards' (1993: 172). In addition to the
bodily sensation of force or pressure, there is also 'the state of
consciously exerting a greater or lesser force with one of your own
limbs' (ibid.). Thus, to quote Peacocke once again, 'it seems that
either sensation or action may each in principle provide routes to
the acquisition of a conception of force (if it is acquired)' (ibid.).

Suppose, next, that it can be shown that sensation and action
are not just possible routes to the acquisition of the concept of
force but that they are the *only* possible routes to the acquisition
of this concept. We can then point out that only an embodied
being could have bodily sensations of force or pressure, or be
conscious of exerting greater or lesser force with one of its own
limbs. It is not just that one must *be* embodied in order to acquire
the concept of force but also that one must be aware of oneself *as*
embodied in order to acquire this concept. In being conscious of
exerting some force with one's body or of the forces acting on
one's body, one cannot fail to be aware of one's own body. One
cannot fail to be aware of oneself as a bodily being. So if bodily
sensation and action are the only possible routes to the acquisition of the concept of force, then awareness of one's own body is,
as BAT implies, a necessary condition for the acquisition of this
concept. I will call this the *acquisition argument* for BAT.[5]

Just as awareness of one's own body might be said to be a necessary condition for the acquisition of the concept of force, so it
might be held that such awareness is also a necessary condition
for the acquisition of other primary quality concepts. For example, Kant suggests in his *Metaphysical Foundations of Natural Science*
that 'by means of the sense of feeling', matter's property of filling
space 'provides us with the size and shape of an extended thing,

[5] There is a brief discussion of this argument in Cassam 1997: 81–3. Strictly speaking,
the acquisition argument is only an argument for one component of BAT, for the claim
that awareness of one's own body is a necessary condition for the acquisition of the
concept of force.

and hence with the concept of a determinate object in space'
(1985: 510). To feel an object is to be in contact with it, and the
contact which is at issue here can only be bodily contact. A closely
related point emerges from Kant's *Anthropology From a Pragmatic
Point of View*. In that work, Kant suggests that nature has given
man the sense of touch so that 'by feeling all the sides of a body
he could form a concept of its shape' (1974: 34). In the absence
of this sense, 'we should be unable to form any concept at all of
the shape of a body' (ibid.). Since tactile awareness of another
body requires awareness of one's own body, this implies that
awareness of one's own body is a necessary condition for the
acquisition of the concept of shape. So here we have another
application of the acquisition argument for BAT.

How good is the acquisition argument? As far as the concept of
force is concerned, one question which this argument raises is
whether bodily sensation and action are possible routes to the
acquisition of the concept of force. Another question is whether
bodily sensation and action are the only possible routes to the
acquisition of the concept of force. On the first of these questions, one difficulty is that primary qualities are supposed to be
mind-independent properties of bodies. One sense in which
primary qualities are mind-independent is that they are properties which exist independently of being perceived. As Locke
describes them, 'they are in the things themselves, whether they
are perceived or no' (1975: 141). Another sense in which primary
qualities are mind-independent is that the things which possess
them need not be, or have, minds. This is another way of saying
that among the things which we usually think of as possessing
primary qualities whether we perceive them or not are inanimate
objects. So if force is a primary quality, then to have the concept
of force is to have the idea of a property which is mind-independent in both of these senses. This means that the bodily sensation
of pressure or consciousness of exerting force with one of one's
own limbs can be the source of our concept of force only if it is
possible to derive the idea of a mind-independent property of
bodies from these sources. The most serious objection to the
acquisition argument is that it fails to explain how this is possible.
It fails to explain how the bodily sensation of pressure can provide
one with the idea of unsensed or unperceived forces. Equally, it
fails to explain how consciousness of exerting force with one of
one's own limbs can give one the idea of forces which are capable
of being exerted by inanimate objects. The problem, it seems, is

that we cannot conceive of forces which no one senses or is conscious of exerting on the model of forces which we do sense or which we are conscious of exerting.[6]

Similar considerations apply to what the acquisition argument says about our acquisition of the concept of shape, for it is difficult to see how feeling all the sides of a body can give one the idea that shapes can exist unfelt. In effect, this is Berkeley's objection to Locke's account of the source of our ideas of primary qualities. Locke thinks that sensation is the source of such ideas but Berkeley's point is that sensation cannot give us the idea of a property of objects which can exist unsensed. Berkeley's conclusion was that the very idea of a primary quality in Locke's sense is unintelligible from an empiricist perspective. The acquisition argument for BAT simply asserts that sensation is a route to the acquisition of concepts of primary qualities but it does not address Berkeley's objection to this proposal. It neither responds to this objection nor attempts to defuse it.

One way of attempting to defuse Berkeley's objection would be to argue that it relies on an unacceptable picture of the nature of experience or sensation. For a better account, it might seem that we need to introduce the idea of an intuitive mechanics.[7] For in order to grasp a primary quality concept, such as shape or mechanical force, it is plausible that one must be capable of engaging in various forms of spatial and mechanical reasoning.[8] In engaging in these forms of reasoning, one must employ the principles of an intuitive or primitive mechanics. For example, one must grasp principles which connect the force which material objects exert with their weight and motion, as well as principles which connect the behaviour of material objects with their shape. On one view, the principles of an intuitive mechanics will also include the principle that primary properties persist through gaps in observation.[9] If this proposal is along the right lines, then one will be able to conceive of primary properties as

---

[6] As Peacocke puts it, if 'a sensitivity to sensations were all that is involved in having a conception of force, conceiving of forces no one experiences would be none too easy a thing to do: you would have to conceive of something felt by no one on the basis of sensations you *do* feel' (1993: 173).

[7] See Peacocke 1993 for more on this idea.

[8] There is an influential defence of this proposal in Evans 1980. Evans argues that in order to grasp the primary properties of matter one must 'master a set of interconnected principles which make up an elementary theory – of primitive mechanics – into which these properties fit and which alone gives them sense' (1980: 95).

[9] See Evans 1980: 95.

capable of existing unperceived as long as one's concepts of such properties are embedded in an intuitive mechanics. Without the appropriate intuitive mechanics, one would not be in a position to make sense of the notion of existence unperceived.

How does any of this help to defuse Berkeley's objection to the view that concepts of primary qualities can be extracted from sensation? One suggestion is that this objection is only compelling if it is read as making the point that concepts of mind-independent properties cannot be extracted from what Peacocke calls 'uninterpreted sensations' (1993: 173). For present purposes, uninterpreted sensations are ones which one could have without already having an intuitive mechanics. In contrast, interpreted sensations presuppose one's possession of an intuitive mechanics. From the fact that concepts of mind-independent properties cannot be extracted from uninterpreted sensations, it should not be concluded that sensation is not a possible route to the acquisition of the concept of force. The correct conclusion is that the sensations from which the concept of force can be extracted must be interpreted sensations. An impoverished conception of the deliverances of sensation is bound to cast doubt on the idea that sensation can be the source of concepts of primary qualities, but the lesson is surely that a viable empiricism must operate with a robust conception of what sensation delivers.

The obvious problem with this line of argument is that it fails to explain our acquisition of those principles of spatial and mechanical reasoning which constitutes one's intuitive mechanics. Since uninterpreted sensations cannot be the source of these principles, it would seem that the only empiricist alternative is to regard interpreted sensations as their source. Yet interpreted sensations are, by definition, such that they presuppose one's possession of an intuitive mechanics. How, in that case, can sensations of this type be the source of one's intuitive mechanics? If interpreted sensations presuppose one's possession of an intuitive mechanics, and one's intuitive mechanics incorporates the idea that there are certain properties which are capable of being perceived and of existing unperceived, then we are none the wiser as to the source of this idea. Indeed, to the extent that neither interpreted nor uninterpreted sensations can be its source, it would be tempting to conclude that it must be an innate idea, and therefore one which does not have its source in experience or sensation.

In fact, this is not quite right. The discussion so far assumes that sensations must either be uninterpreted or internally connected with an intuitive mechanics, but these are not the only possibilities. Another possibility would be to view sensations as intrinsically intentional or representational psychological occurrences which do not presuppose one's possession of an intuitive mechanics. Understood in this way, sensations represent objects as possessors of mind-independent primary qualities such as force and shape, but it is possible for sensations to have this representational content even if they are not, in Peacocke's sense, interpreted. If uninterpreted sensations are not intrinsically intentional, then it is no surprise that concepts of mind-independent primary qualities cannot be extracted from them. If, on the other hand, uninterpreted sensations are representations of mind-independent primary qualities and are uninterpreted only in the sense that they are enjoyable without any prior grasp of an intuitive mechanics, then it is no longer a mystery how they can provide a route to the acquisition of concepts of such qualities. On this interpretation, the sense in which many empiricists operate with an unacceptably impoverished conception of what sensation delivers is not that they fail to see that sensations must be interpreted. It is that they fail to see that sensations can be representational without presupposing our possession of the very concepts whose acquisition empiricism is attempting to explain.

The question which now arises is whether we really understand how sensations which are 'enjoyable without possession of an intuitive mechanics' (Peacocke 1993: 172) can be genuinely representational. Suppose that we think of interpreted sensations as ones whose representational content is a form of conceptual content.[10] In these terms, what I have just been suggesting is that it is sensations whose content is representational without being conceptual which provide a route to the formation of concepts of mind-independent primary qualities. So what is now needed is, among other things, a defence of the view that there can be non-conceptual representational content. Perhaps the most promising defence of this view from an empiricist perspective would be to point out that it is only intelligible that concepts can be derived

---

[10] For present purposes, the representational content of an experience or sensation is conceptual if its subject must possess those concepts which are required to specify its content. Its content is non-conceptual if the concepts required to specify its content are ones which are not, or need not be, possessed by its subject. For more on the notion of non-conceptual representational content, see Evans 1982, Bermúdez 1998, and Peacocke 2001.

from experience or sensation if we suppose that not all sensory content is conceptual.[11] In particular, unless we are prepared to view concepts of primary qualities as innate, we must concede that there are experiences which do not presuppose them. This is just another way of saying that we must concede that the representational content of experience need not be wholly conceptual.

This amounts to a transcendental argument to the effect that the existence of non-conceptual representational content is a necessary condition for concepts, including concepts of primary qualities, to be derivable from experience. One worry about this argument is that it begs an important question by assuming that concepts of primary qualities are derivable from experience. Another is that the transcendental argument does not explain how intrinsically intentional sensations can be non-conceptual. It argues that there must be sensations which are both representational and non-conceptual but it does not say how this is possible. For example, it does not explain how sensations of pressure which are enjoyable without any prior grasp of an intuitive mechanics can represent sensed forces as capable of existing unsensed. To this extent, the transcendental argument for non-conceptual representational content cannot be the end of the story, even if one grants its empiricist presuppositions.

Any serious account of the nature and possibility of non-conceptual representational content would need to address questions in the theory of content which go well beyond the scope of the present discussion. As far as this discussion is concerned, the important point to have emerged is that if it makes sense to think of sensations as non-conceptual representations of primary qualities, then Berkeley's objection to the acquisition argument is inconclusive. In principle, we can still think of concepts of primary qualities as formed from sensations as long as we refrain from thinking of sensations either as non-representational or as presupposing concepts of primary qualities. From an empiricist perspective, what is controversial about the acquisition argument for BAT is not its assumption that the concept of force can be acquired from sensation or action but its assertion that awareness of one's own body is a necessary condition for the acquisition of this concept. So the question which now needs to be addressed is whether bodily sensation and action are the only possible routes to the acquisition of the concept of force.

---

[11] For a closely related line of argument, see Bermúdez 1998: 58–62.

Empiricists who are sceptical about BAT might argue that action cannot be a strictly necessary condition for the acquisition of the concept of force since what H.H. Price calls a 'purely contemplative being' (1932: 275), one that is incapable of physical action, might still be capable of acquiring this concept. A common reaction to this proposal is to insist that such a being could only acquire the concept of force as long as it can still experience bodily sensations of force or pressure. But now suppose that its nerves are damaged in such a way that it cannot experience bodily sensations of force. If, in the absence of such sensations, a purely contemplative being can still acquire the concept of force, then it is doubtful whether awareness of one's own body is a strictly necessary condition for the acquisition of this concept.

How exactly is a purely contemplative being which lacks sensations of force supposed to have acquired the concept of force? Suppose that we agree with the mechanist that the force of a body in motion is exercised or manifested when it collides with another body, thereby causing a change in the state of motion of that other body. On the assumption that even a purely contemplative being can still see other bodies as colliding and deflecting, a natural suggestion would be that this amounts to a purely visual experience of mechanical force, a type of experience from which the concept of mechanical force can be extracted even by creatures which lack awareness of their own bodies. What we have here, therefore, is an apparent counterexample to the thesis that awareness of one's own body is essentially involved in *all* of the different kinds of experience from which the concept of force can be derived. The most that can plausibly be said is that awareness of one's own body is involved in *some* of the experiences from which this concept can be derived.

A Humean response to this line of argument would be to object that the concept of force is not exemplified in visual experience, but this response does not seem to be correct. We can indeed see objects as exerting and being subject to mechanical forces. To borrow an example of Strawson's, 'in a great boulder rolling down the mountainside and flattening the wooden hut in its path we see an exemplary instance of force' (1992: 118). In the light of this and other such examples, it would not be plausible to insist that the concept of force is not exemplified in visual experience. And if the concept of force is exemplified in visual experience, then there is no reason to deny that the concept of force can be extracted from visual experience.

The suggestion that the concept of force can be extracted from visual experience only poses a threat to BAT on the assumption that visual experience does not presuppose awareness of one's own body. This assumption is, however, open to question since it is arguable that there is no such thing as a visual experience which does not involve some awareness of one's body. Visual experience involves visual sensations, and visual sensations are, like all sensations, bodily occurrences. More generally, as Ayers remarks, our visual awareness of things in space 'involves some awareness of the relation which they bear to the part of us from which we see', and this awareness is 'integrated with, indeed involves, our general tactile and proprioceptive awareness of the head and its relation to the rest of the body' (1991: 187). The fact that the concept of force can be extracted from visual experience therefore poses no immediate threat to BAT.

It also needs to be recognized that sight is normally integrated with the other senses and with the capacity for action. This leads to the idea that only a creature with a sense of touch and the ability consciously to exert force with its own body can properly be said to see other bodies as exerting and being subject to mechanical forces. The suggestion here is that if it were not for one's own bodily engagement with the world, there would be nothing in virtue of which it would be correct to say that force enters into the intentional content of visual experience. The intentional content of visual experience is, to this extent, determined by the complex relations that exist between visual perception and our other perceptual and active capacities. On this account, a being which has no bodily engagement with the world would have no impression of force, not even a purely visual impression. In contrast, we can see objects as exerting and being subject to mechanical forces because mechanical force is not something which we are only aware of visually.

According to this line of argument, there is good reason to question the coherence of the hypothesis of a purely contemplative being that has no awareness of its own body but which is still capable of enjoying visual experiences which resemble the visual experiences which we enjoy. Our visual experiences are, in the first instance, experiences with spatial content, and the spatial objects which we are aware of as such are, for the most part, also ones which we can touch. As Merleau-Ponty puts it, 'visible and tangible belong to the same world', and 'every vision takes place somewhere in the tactile space' (1968: 134). To imagine a being with no awareness of its own body is to imagine a being with no sense of touch and no capacity for physical action. To imagine a being with no sense of touch and no capacity for physical action is, however, to imagine a being whose visual experiences would be quite unlike ours. Indeed, it is open to question whether such a being could even be said to have visual experiences with determinate spatial content, let alone visual experiences which present themselves as experiences of force. So we should not make the mistake of taking the fact that our visual experiences have a certain intentional content to show that a being with no awareness of its own body could have visual experiences with the same intentional content.

In arguing in this way, it should not be forgotten that there are actual human beings who suffer from various forms of what might be called 'body-blindness'. There is, for example, the well-documented case of a person who has no touch or proprioception below the neck but who is apparently still capable of seeing the world more or less as the rest of us do.[12] Yet this is still not a case of someone with no awareness of his own body seeing the world as we do. The subject in this case is only partially body blind and can still act in the world. He can lift things and is aware of the effort which he puts into doing so. He has the concept of force, but there is no reason to suppose that his route to this concept did not involve awareness of his own body. So BAT remains intact.

The thesis for which I have been arguing is similar to a thesis for which W. Joske argues in his book *Material Objects*. Joske's thesis is that 'our appreciation of the fact that we live in a world in which material things are common is dependent upon awareness of our own body' (1967: 18). The basis of this thesis is the thought that solidity or impenetrability is the defining property of matter, and that we are aware of solid objects 'because we can move our limbs and body, and know that such movements are being resisted' (ibid.). In response to the suggestion that an inactive being with the sense of sight could still be visually aware of impenetrability just as we are, Joske argues that this presupposes that such a being already has the *concept* of solidity. This concept might be available to an inactive being, but only if it has the capacity to feel sensations of pressure and collision. To this extent, it remains the case, according to Joske, that 'without an awareness of our own body, at least as the seat of sensations, we would have

---

[12] The case which I have in mind is the one described in Cole 1991.

no proper concept of solidity at all' (1967: 20), and so would be unable to detect solidity with our eyes.

Much of this is highly congenial to what I am arguing here, but there are important differences. One important difference is that the emphasis in Joske's account of what it is to be a material object is on the notion of solidity rather than that of force. Another difference is that on Joske's account only someone with the concept of solidity can see things as solid. Since I do not wish to commit myself to the view that intentional content is conceptual, my claim is not that only someone with the concept of force can see things as exerting and being subject to forces. For Joske, seeing objects as material requires awareness of one's own body because awareness of one's own body is required to establish the concept of solidity. On my view, seeing objects as material requires awareness of one's own body because awareness of one's own body is part and parcel of the other perceptual and active capacities with which the capacity to see objects as material must be integrated. Awareness of one's own body is required to establish the concept of force, but this is not the basis of my proposal that seeing objects as material requires awareness of one's body.

Before concluding this phase of my discussion, there is one more issue which needs to be addressed. At several points in my exposition of the acquisition argument for BAT, I have referred to the possibility of regarding concepts of primary qualities as innate. A concept is innate just if it is possessed without having been acquired.[13] Since innate concepts have not been acquired, they have not been acquired from experience. So even if it is true that bodily awareness is a necessary condition for the *acquisition* of concepts of primary qualities from experience, it does not follow from this that bodily awareness is a necessary condition for the *possession* of such concepts. This does not follow because these concepts might be possessed without having been acquired. And if bodily awareness is not a necessary condition for possession of concepts of primary qualities, then it would seem that awareness of one's own body is not a necessary condition for thinking of objects as material.

One thing that might be said in response to this line of argument is that the best case for regarding a given concept as innate is that we cannot understand how that concept could have been

---

[13] This characterization of what it would be for a concept to be innate is drawn from Bennett 1966: 98.

acquired from experience. Hence, as long as the notion of non-conceptual representational content makes it intelligible that concepts of primary qualities can be derived from experience, this counts against the view that these concept are innate. Still, it must be conceded that nothing that I have said shows that it would be strictly incoherent to regard concepts of primary qualities as innate. The lesson is that a convincing argument for BAT cannot content itself with pointing out that awareness of one's own body is essentially involved in those kinds of experience from which it is possible to acquire the concept of force. The acquisition argument for BAT might convince empiricists who believe that the concept of force must be acquired, but it should not convince nativists who think that this concept is not, or need not be, acquired.

It would be helpful to remember at this point that BAT is not just the thesis that awareness of one's own body is a necessary condition for the acquisition of concepts of primary qualities. It is also the thesis that awareness of one's own body is a necessary condition for the possession of concepts of primary qualities. If this were not the case, BAT would not licence the conclusion that awareness of one's own body is a necessary condition for thinking of objects as material. If, on the other hand, awareness of one's own body turns out to be a necessary condition for the possession of concepts of primary qualities, then even nativists must concede that a thinker with no awareness of her own body would be unable to think of objects as material.

In brief, the case for insisting that possession of concepts like force and shape requires awareness of one's own body is this: like other concepts of primary qualities, these are concepts which someone who has them must be in a position to apply on the basis of experience. This means that a thinker who has shape concepts must be able to perceive the shape of things and apply the appropriate shape concept on the basis of her experiences of shape. Equally, possession of the concept of force is bound up with the capacity to perceive or exert some degree of force. There are, of course, concepts which are not tied to experience in this way, but one's concepts of primary qualities would lack what Kant calls *objective reality* if it were not for the fact that instances of them are given as such in experience.

This is the point at which awareness of one's own body comes into the picture. In the acquisition argument for BAT, awareness of one's own body figures as an essential component of those experiences from which concepts of primary qualities are acquired. The present suggestion is that awareness of one's own body is an essential component of those experiences of primary qualities which provide one's concepts of primary qualities with objective reality. A thinker who has never had any experience of shape or force is one who has no proper conception of shape or force. The point is that there are ways of thinking about shape and force which are, as Peacocke remarks, 'made available by certain kinds of conscious experience' (1993: 173). Thinkers who lack these kinds of conscious experience cannot think in these ways, and thinkers who cannot think in these ways cannot be credited with concepts of these primary qualities. In deference to Kant, I will call this the *objective reality argument* for BAT.

Among the many questions raised by this argument, one concerns the validity of the objective reality requirement itself. Concepts have objective reality if and only if they have 'application to objects which can be given to us in intuition' (B150).[14] Kant's proposal is that concepts which cannot, in this sense, be 'made sensible' (A240/ B299) are empty or insignificant. Although some concepts which lack objective reality might retain a meaning which is 'purely logical' (A147/ B186), the meaning of concepts of primary qualities cannot be purely logical.[15] In the absence of any relation to experience, they would be 'without *sense*' (A240/ B299).[16] This is not to deny that a thinker might lose her ability to experience primary qualities while retaining her concepts of such qualities. To this extent, we can allow that a thinker who gets into a state of body-blindness or total sensory deprivation might retain her ability to think of objects as material. But it only makes sense to think of someone *retaining* an ability if she had it in the first place, and the point of the objective reality requirement is to insist that one cannot grasp concepts of primary qualities without ever having been in a position to experience their instances.

The implication of this discussion is that the sense in which awareness of one's own body is a necessary condition for thinking of objects as material is not that one must *always* be aware of one's own body in order to think of objects as material. The suggestion is

[14] All references in this form are to Kant 1933.

[15] In the Schematism, the concepts which Kant describes as retaining a purely logical meaning 'even after elimination of every sensible condition' (A147/ B186) are the categories.

[16] The concepts which Kant is discussing at this point are those of mathematics.

rather that in order to think of objects as material, one must *sometimes* be aware of one's own body. This is so because one cannot think of objects as material unless one has concepts of primary qualities, one cannot have concepts of primary qualities without any experience of primary qualities, and one cannot experience primary qualities without any awareness of one's own body. As far as the objective reality argument is concerned, this is the best that can be done for BAT. It is one thing to draw attention to the connections that exist between experience, bodily awareness and concepts of primary qualities, but proponents of BAT must also be careful not to exaggerate the tightness of these connections.

To sum up, I have considered two arguments for BAT, the acquisition argument and the objective reality argument. Neither argument is unproblematic and it has also emerged that BAT is, in some ways, a more modest thesis than it might have appeared at the outset. Nevertheless, the concessions made by the acquisition and objective reality arguments should not be allowed to obscure the central point of this discussion. The central point is that there is a complex story to be told about what is involved in the acquisition and grasp of concepts of primary qualities, and that neither our acquisition nor our grasp of these concepts can be satisfactorily accounted for without reference to our awareness of our own bodies. It is this awareness which, in conjunction with many other cognitive capacities, provides us with a concrete sense of the kind of world which we inhabit.

III

The remaining issue is whether we can think of our own bodies as material objects. In so far as awareness of one's own body is required in order to think of objects as material, it is also required in order to think of one's own body as material. To think of one's own body as a material object is to think of it as a bearer of primary qualities and as a thing among other things. The first of these requirements is easily fulfilled. For example, there is little difficulty in thinking of one's own body as shaped and as exerting and being subject to mechanical forces. There is little difficulty in thinking of one's body in these terms because the forms of awareness which provide one with concepts of such primary qualities are also forms of awareness which provide one with a sense of one's body as shaped and as exerting and being subject to mechanical forces. For to be conscious of sensations of force is to be conscious of one's own body as something which is subject to force. To be conscious of exerting force with one's limbs is to be conscious of one's own body as an exerter of mechanical force. In each of these respects, one is conscious of one's own body as a locus of mechanical force and is thereby in a position to think of it as a material object.

A more difficult question is whether one can think of one's own body as a thing among other things, a material object among material objects. The problem is to reconcile the idea that one's body is a thing among other things with its role in sensation and perception. Among those who think that these two aspects of one's own body cannot be reconciled in one's thought about it is Sartre. He claims that one's body is either 'a thing among other things, or it is that by which things are revealed to me. But it cannot be both at the same time' (1989: 304). In other words, in representing one's own body as a subject of perception and sensation, one deprives oneself of the means to represent it as an object among others in the world. By the same token, one deprives oneself of the means to represent it as a material object.

One response to this argument would be to deny that it makes sense to regard one's own body as a subject of sensation and perception. Sensations, including those of force and pressure, certainly present themselves as having a bodily location, but this is not the same thing as saying that one's own body is, or presents itself as being, the bearer or subject of such sensations. As for the idea that one's body is something which sees and touches, as well as something which can be seen and touched, it might be objected that one's body is not literally the subject of one's visual and tactile perception. One's body is only what one uses in order to perceive the surrounding world, but it is not that which perceives the surrounding world. As long as one's body is thought of as an instrument rather than as a subject of perception, there is no problem reconciling its role in perception with the idea that it is a thing among other things.

Someone who argues in this way can agree that there is a sense in which my body is that by which things are revealed to me. The present suggestion is that the sense in which this is so does not make it difficult to think of one's body as a material object. After all, even a Cartesian can accept that my body is that by which things are revealed to me without accepting that my body is the subject to which the things which I perceive reveal themselves. For Descartes, one's body is something possessed by the subject of one's experiences. Unlike the subject itself, it can easily be thought of as a material object, as a thing among other things and as a bearer of primary qualities. It is true that in experiencing sensations of force or in being conscious of exerting force with one's own limbs one cannot fail to be aware of oneself as embodied, but being aware of oneself as embodied need not be a matter of being aware of one's thinking, perceiving self as a material object.

Although I will not attempt to make the case here, I believe that this line of argument is mistaken and that it is indeed appropriate to think of one's own body as that which perceives the surrounding world rather than as a mere instrument of perception. What makes it difficult to think of one's body as that which perceives the surrounding world and as a bearer of sensations is the idea that one's body is a 'mere' body, a piece of inanimate physical matter. On this account, a purely instrumental conception of the role of the body in sensation and perception is hard to avoid. There is, however, an alternative to this way of thinking. The alternative is to insist that that which sees and touches is not a mere body but a living human body.[17] It is one's living body which can coherently be thought of as a constituent of one's subjectivity, as a point of occupancy for psychological properties. Yet, contrary to what Sartre maintains, the thought that one's living body belongs to the subjective order and is in this sense that by which things are revealed to me does not preclude the thought that this body is also a thing among other things. It does not preclude the thought that one's living body is a material object among material objects.

The possibility of thinking of one's living body both as a subject and as a thing among other things is one to which Merleau-Ponty draws attention when he describes our body as 'a being of two leaves, from one side a thing among things and otherwise what sees and touches them' (1968: 137). The suggestion that one's body has a 'double belongingness to the order of the "object" and to the order of the "subject" ' (ibid.) is Merleau-Ponty's suggestive gloss on the idea that one's body is a sensible sentient or what he describes elsewhere as a 'subject-object' (1989: 95). In so far as one's sentient body is

---

[17] For more on this alternative, see Cassam 1997: 56–61.

what sees and touches, its role in perception is not just that of an instrument. In so far as it belongs to the objective order, it is a thing among other things. The mistake is to assume that it cannot be both at the same time.

I would not wish to suggest that these brief remarks constitute an adequate defence of the thesis that our bodies belong to the order of the subject and to the order of the object. The suggestion that our bodies, even our living bodies, belong to the order of the subject is one which is likely to meet with especially strong resistance. For present purposes, however, the more important claim is that our bodies belong to the order of the object, and that this is so even if they also belong to the order of the subject. If they do not belong to the order of the subject, then so much the worse for those who maintain that we cannot think of our bodies as objects among others in the world.

The position, then, is that whether one conceives of one's body as something which one uses to perceive the surrounding world or as that which perceives the surrounding world, there is no good reason to suppose that it cannot properly be regarded as a thing among other things. To this extent, there is no good reason to suppose that it cannot properly be regarded as a material object. As I have been emphasizing, the interesting and difficult question is not whether one can conceive of one's body as a material object but whether the forms of bodily awareness which make this conception available to us are ones which someone who possesses concepts of primary qualities can coherently be supposed to lack. If what I have been arguing is correct, then, with allowances for the possibility of partial or temporary body-blindness, this question should be answered in the negative.

References

Ayers, M. R. (1991). *Locke, vol. I: Epistemology* (London: Routledge).

Bennett, J. (1966). *Kant's Analytic* (Cambridge: Cambridge University Press).

Bermúdez, J. L. (1998). *The Paradox of Self-Consciousness* (Cambridge, Mass.: The MIT Press).

Cassam, Q. (1997). *Self and World* (Oxford: Clarendon Press).

Cole, J. (1991). *Pride and a Daily Marathon* (London: Duckworth).

Eilan, N. McCarthy, R., and Brewer, B. (1993) (eds.). *Spatial Representation* (Oxford: Basil Blackwell).

Evans, G. (1980). 'Things Without the Mind – A Commentary upon Chapter Two of Strawson's *Individuals*', in Van Straaten (1980), 76–116.

Evans, G. (1982). *The Varieties of Reference*, edited by J. McDowell (Oxford: Oxford University Press).

Joske, W. (1967). *Material Objects* (London: Macmillan).

Kant, I. (1933). *Critique of Pure Reason*, trans. Norman Kemp Smith (London: Macmillan).

Kant, I. (1974). *Anthropology From A Pragmatic Point of View*, trans. Mary J. Gregor (The Hague: Martinus Nijhoff).

Kant, I. (1985). *Metaphysical Foundations of Natural Science*, trans. James W. Ellington (Indianapolis: Hackett Publishing Company).

Locke, J. (1975). *An Essay Concerning Human Understanding*, edited by P. H. Nidditch (Oxford: Clarendon Press).

Merleau-Ponty, M. (1968). *The Visible and the Invisible*, trans. Alphonso Lingis (Evanston: Northwestern University Press).

Peacocke, C. (1993). 'Intuitive Mechanics, Psychological Reality, and the Idea of a Material Object', in Eilan, N. McCarthy, R., and Brewer, B. (1993), 162–76.

Peacocke, C. (2001). 'Does Perception Have a Nonconceptual Content?', *Journal of Philosophy*, XCVIII: 239–64.

Price, H. H. (1932). *Perception* (London: Methuen).

Sartre, J.-P. (1989). *Being and Nothingness*, trans. Hazel Barnes (London: Routledge).

Strawson, P.F. (1992). *Analysis and Metaphysics: An Introduction to Philosophy* (Oxford: Oxford University Press).

Van Straaten, Z. (1980) (ed.). *Philosophical Subjects: Essays Presented to P. F. Strawson* (Oxford: Clarendon Press).

Warren, D. (2001). 'Kant's Dynamics', in Watkins (2001), 93–116.

Watkins, E. (2001) (ed.). *Kant and the Sciences* (Oxford: Oxford University Press).

2

CORPOREAL OBJECTS AND THE INTERDEPENDENCE OF PERCEPTION AND ACTION

Maximilian de Gaynesford

Hamlet eventually takes arms against his sea of troubles and thus acquires sufficient self-knowledge to end them. Staple motifs of homespun wisdom collude with the moral of that tale: the inactive cannot hope to gain self-knowledge. A long philosophical tradition, which can claim George Berkeley as a most effective member,[1] puts the matter more technically: self-awareness in *any* form is dependent on the exercise of agency. What drives this tradition is the belief that perceptual experience alone is insufficient to provide for self-awareness:

> Perceptual experience alone is powerless to place its subject with respect to its objects... It is rather that perceptual contents are self-locating in virtue of their contribution to the subject's capacity for basic purposive action in the world.[2]

The positive heart of this paper upholds the opposed view. Certain forms of perceptual experience – bodily awareness – are sufficient to provide one with (introspective) self-awareness. This claim is consistent with the existence of plausible constitutive interdependence relations between the exercise of agency and self-awareness at *certain* levels, as I shall indicate.

My secondary purpose in this paper is to question certain kinds of motivation for adopting the position advocated in the quotation above. The position is grounded in one type of self-awareness in particular: the way in which one's perceptual experience locates one spatially in the world – i.e. what has been called *egocentric spatial perception*. We may distinguish two claims at issue.

---

[1] G. Berkeley, *Three dialogues between Hylas and Philonous* [1713] (Oxford: OUP, 1998), p. 117.

[2] B. Brewer 'Self-location and agency', *Mind*, 101, (1992), p. 26.

The Strong Dependence Thesis (SDT): The egocentric spatial perception of corporeal objects requires that they perceive and exercise their agency in their environment.

SDT is false, I believe: some corporeal objects who choose not to (or are unable to) exercise agency in their environment are nevertheless capable of egocentric spatial perception.

The Insufficiency Claim: Perceptual experience is insufficient to provide for self-awareness.

This claim is both stronger and weaker than *SDT*. It is stronger because it covers all forms of self-awareness, not just egocentric spatial perception. It is weaker because it does not specify what is required to supplement or replace perceptual experience. Indeed, it is consistent with the *Insufficiency Claim* to deny that it is *agency* that must supplement perception if self-awareness is to be provided for.

The *Insufficiency Claim* is false, I shall claim, for reasons that have to do with my positive proposal. Since certain forms of bodily awareness count as perceptual experiences, introspective self-awareness may be provided for by perceptual experiences alone.

Egocentric spatial perception

It has been said that we should *define* 'egocentric space' in terms of action:

The axes distinctive of an egocentric frame are those that are immediately used by the subject in the direction of action.[3]

But this begs the question in favour of *SDT*; so the definition should be amended.

Standardly, we experience the world as containing ourselves, an experience that locates us spatially in relation to other things the world contains. For example, you are holding this page before you now; you see it at a certain distance from you; you are more or less in front of it, nearer or further away, to its left or right, according to where it is and where you are. If you look around you, your perceptual experience will be similar. In seeing, hearing and touching other objects within the perceptual field, you will be

---

[3] J. Campbell, *Past, Space and Self* (Cambridge: MIT Press, 1994), p. 14.

experiencing them as spatially related to you and you will be experiencing yourself as located within this field. In short, we perceive the world in an egocentric spatial way.

But how is egocentric spatial perception possible? One might think there is no mystery – at least if we assume, as I shall throughout, that the self is a particular living human being. For then, whether or not the self is identical with the body,[4] it is at least a material object,[5] extended in space and enduring through time, which is either impenetrably solid or force-exerting.[6] We perceive the world as containing many such corporeal objects. So why should one more be a problem? Indeed, one seems to be perceptually aware of the corporeal object *one* is as the object of one's perceptions. The phenomenon occurs frequently and not only visually. As I speak, I am acquiring perceptual information about the corporeal object I am – through my eyes, ears, hands, nose and tongue. There may be an interesting disanalogy here with the way I perceive other bodies etc, but not such as to undermine the claim that I nevertheless perceive the corporeal object I am.

Some appear to begrudge admitting the point; they claim that being an object of one's perceptions is the exception rather than the rule.[7] There is a sense in which it is right to be cautious here. It is indeed exceptional to be perceptually aware of the object one is as something that is merely *in fact* oneself – e.g. catching a reflection in a mirror – i.e. an object that may surprise or even

---

[4] The Strawsonian person is not identical with the body, but is nevertheless included in the assumption – it is a 'corporeal object'. Cf. P. Strawson, *Individuals* (London: Methuen and Co, 1959).

[5] By 'material objects' I mean items which do not exist in virtue of being perceived; which cannot be in their entirety located in two places at one time; which possibly move; which are the nexus of certain causal relations; which are internally causally connected over time, having an inherent tendency to retain their current properties or to change them in various ways; and which, externally, are the possible causes of various kinds of phenomena as a consequence of being interrelated with other objects. See Hoffman and Rosenkrantz, *Substance* (London: Routledge, 1997), pp. 4–5; Campbell (1994), pp. 25–36.

[6] Solidity, understood as impenetrability (the utter exclusion of one body by another; not merely its displacement), is Locke's criterion: 'impenetrability ... of all other, seems the idea most intimately connected with, and essential to body'. J. Locke, *An Essay concerning Human Understanding* [1689] ed. P. H. Nidditch (Oxford: Oxford University Press, 1975), II.4.1. Being force-exerting is Leibniz's criterion, later picked up by Kant: 'the essence of a body ... is to be located in the power of acting and resisting alone'. G. W. Leibniz, *Philosophical Writings*, ed. G. H. R. Parkinson (London: Dent, 1973), p. 82. But I shall not investigate the issue. Whether or not the primary properties of mass, weight, position, size, shape, and motion must be ascribable to an item if it is to count as a *body* (as the Lockean account would suggest), they are certainly necessary if that item is to count as a living human being.

[7] E.g. Brewer (1992), p. 19.

horrify one in *turning out to be* oneself.[8] If this is the exception, what is the rule? Here is a tempting suggestion: generally speaking, it is as *oneself* that one is perceptually aware of the corporeal object one is. It is not *wrong* to say one is perceptually aware of *the object one is* as the object of one's perceptions; for that is a locution covering rule and exception. But it is misleading; in capturing the exception, it suggests the exception is the rule.

If it is as *oneself* that one is generally perceptually aware of the corporeal object one is, it can seem that one is perceptually aware of that object as the *subject* of one's perception. Hence there is something special about the corporeal object one is: it is the object doing the perceiving. So the question arises with respect to egocentric spatial perception: how can it be that the object one is, the object doing the perceiving, perceives *itself* alongside other objects, locates *itself* in relation to them, and is contained with them in the same world? How can the object one is be both the *object* of one's awareness and, at the same time, its *subject?*

Constitutive interdependence

It seems plausible to answer: by virtue of a constitutive interdependence between one's perceiving of the world and one's exercising one's agency in it. This position is attractive for a number of reasons; three are worth noting.

A constitutive interdependence between agency and perception sits nicely with one's experience as an egocentric spatial perceiver. For it is generally by making use of various combinations of action and perception that one investigates the world. One observes while walking; stops to scrutinise something more minutely and accurately; moves forward again and to the side to discover further features of some focal object; and so on. Moreover, as an egocentric spatial perceiver, one commonly experiences oneself both as a perceiver and as an agent. One is aware not just of *what* one perceives, but often of *perceiving* what one perceives; if this were not the case, it would be difficult to explain how we are sometimes surprised at what we experience. One is also aware not just of what one's actions achieve, but how to act in

---

[8] John Banville offers a particularly keen description of this phenomenon: 'In the street I would catch sight of my reflection in a shop window, skulking along with head down and shoulders up and my elbows pressed into my sides, like a felon bearing a body away, and I would falter, and almost fall, breathless as if from a blow, overwhelmed by the inescapable predicament of being what I was'. *Eclipse* (London: Picador, 2000), p. 88.

order to secure those achievements. And this may be connected to the fact that one is aware of oneself in ways that one is not aware of others – an awareness *'from the inside'* as some say. One has to look to know what others are doing with their bodies, for example, but one usually knows what one's own fingers are doing without having to look.

A constitutive interdependence between agency and perception in the particular case of egocentric spatial perception is nicely in line with current revisionism about perception and action more generally. Philosophers and psychologists now decry the 'bad old' view of the mind according to which perception and action are quite distinct, the one figuring as input to the mind and the other as its output.[9] On this old view, the mind receives sensory information from its environment, information which is then given structure by various cognitive processes and fed into the motor cortex to produce action. This view seems erroneous for numerous neurophysiological, behavioural and philosophical reasons.[10] We should, instead, treat perception and action as constitutively interdependent.[11]

Finally, it is often claimed that perceptual experience is insufficient to provide for self-awareness. There are various versions of this *Insufficiency Claim.* If it is correct, we nevertheless have to find some way of accounting for egocentric spatial perception, a way that gives *some* role to perception. And *SDT* looks promising here. For it allows the self to be encountered perceptually but not *purely* perceptually – i.e. in virtue of the combinatory exercise of agency and perception.

It is with this third way of motivating constitutive interdependence

---

[9] Susan Hurley, *Consciousness in Action* (London: Harvard University Press, 1998) offers a representative discussion.

[10] It distinguishes in an arbitrary manner between the motor and sensory cortices. It treats perception as wholly passive when it should be regarded as part of the organism's active preparation to respond. It ignores the extent to which movement is part of the perceptual process, crucially important, for example, in effecting the parallax by which environmental objects are presented geometrically to a sufficient specification and degree of accuracy. It treats action as an effect of perception when it is as much a cause. It portrays the relations between action and perception as instrumental when action has a controlling role over perception and is neither stimulus-driven nor wholly autonomous. It treats the causal flow between action and perception as linear – from world to sensory system to perception to cognition to motor systems to action to world again – when it is a dynamic feedback process.

[11] It should be said that such revision has tended to overlook complications that are nevertheless crucial features of our concept of perception: e.g. that someone enjoying the experiences perception has to offer should be able to see, hear, touch, taste and smell something yet do nothing.

that I shall now raise difficulties. The position itself is attractive; but for the other reasons given.

Patient perceivers

Consider the following argument for *SDT*. We perceive the world in a self-locating way – i.e. there is some local holism between the way we perceive objects as spatially related to us and the way we locate ourselves in relation to those objects that provides for an awareness expressible in first-personal terms by saying 'that F is to my right, behind me, above me' etc. This would not be possible unless there were an 'interrelation between perception and action' constituting 'a kind of triangulation of the subject's location in the single world of each'.[12] So it is a necessary condition of perceiving the world in a self-locating way that the perceiver be an agent exercising his agency on the perceived environment.[13]

If this is correct, then the perceptual experience of anyone who is not exercising their agency on the perceived environment is not self-locating. This is frankly amazing.[14] Odysseus was still picking himself out perceptually in relation to other objects he was experiencing when bound to the mast of his ship and sailing past the rock on which the sirens sang. Someone paralysed for a time has that capacity when being wheeled around on a hospital bed. And so, presumably, has someone paralysed from birth—i.e. someone who may always have been incapable of acting on the

---

[12] Brewer (1992) provides a clear expression of the argument. 'Perceptual experience alone is powerless to place its subject with respect to its objects... It is rather that perceptual contents are self-locating in virtue of their contribution to the subject's capacity for basic purposive action in the world. This mutually shaping psychological relation places the subject in the perceived world by bringing its objects into his environment as the focus of his perceptually controlled behaviour. At the same time, it maintains a fundamental separation between himself and the rest of the world in virtue of the direct practical awareness he has of the special status of his body as the *immediate* respondent to his will. It is therefore this role of experience in focussing and guiding world-directed action which justifies the self-locating spatial structure in perceptual contents' (1992, pp. 26–7).

[13] Note that the appeal of such arguments – of which the quotation from Brewer is representative – usually rests on regarding perception and action as discrete: each has its 'world'; the one provides a second and mutually-solving route to the other's locating of self. Consequently, such arguments will not persuade those who think the two are constitutively interdependent. If this latter view of the mind is correct, it would make no sense either to affirm or deny the question arguments such as Brewer's make central: whether or not self-location is 'purely perceptual'. But I shall not pursue the point: it would take us too far from present concerns and local objections.

[14] As Q. Cassam notes: 'The connections between egocentric spatial perception and action are surely not so tight as to exclude the possibility of someone paralysed from birth seeing things as being in specific directions from her.' *Self and World* (Oxford: OUP, 1997), p. 85.

perceived environment, though they may be capable of engaging in mental actions.

This objection might be called 'the problem of patient perceivers' – the case of perceivers who are acted *against* rather than acting. For it seems one might be the subject or object of mere activity and nevertheless one's perceptions (continue to) be self-locating. This is contrary to *SDT*, of course, because being the subject or object of mere activity is not sufficient for one to be said to be exercising one's agency on the perceived environment. Thus the problem of patient perceivers undermines *SDT*.

First response

It might be said that the perceptually self-locating subjects in these examples are in fact exercising their agency over the perceived environment – *if 'agency' is loosely interpreted.*

This response is predicated on the idea that the phrase 'exercising one's agency on the perceived environment' has been interpreted in a more restrictive sense than is normal or justified. But there is little to be said for this option, I think.

What I have said so far is consistent with the remarkably *unrestrictive* view that x is exercising its agency just in case x does little more than possess and exercise a power to make something happen. It is consistent, in other words, with the existence of inanimate agents and unintentional agency – e.g. with saying that oxygen is an agent when it rusts metal, or that birds are agents when they build nests. Compare this with a fairly standard view that would evidently exclude these possibilities:

> Action does require that what the agent does is intentional under some description, and this in turn requires ... that what the agent does is known to him under some description.[15]

Second response

It might be objected that the perceptually self-locating subjects in these examples are in fact exercising their agency over the perceived environment – *if SDT is loosely interpreted.*

The response comes to this. *SDT* itself permits 'agency' to be

---

[15] Davidson, *Essays on actions and events* (Oxford: OUP, 1980), p. 50.

interpreted less restrictively than is normal. Once freed of restrictiveness in one or other direction, we can allow that the examples actually illustrate agency in the relevant sense.

The main problem with this option is that, if we weaken what is required by *SDT* so that the examples I have mentioned may be admitted, it will no longer be a claim about *agency* at all. But there are various further worries worth mentioning about this option.

Suppose we adopt the following definition:

(a) 'x is exercising its agency just in case x is active'.[16]

The problem is that x may be active without exercising agency. For x may be active given only that x is not passive; and x need not be exercising its agency over the perceived environment to be non-passive. For example, one might be engaged merely in mental actions of a restricted sort (like solving a Maths problem). Or one might be acted against rather than acting (like being moved or shown around). Or things might befall or impinge on one that have nothing to do with agency (like being receptive to the perceptual flow). Or one might be engaged in reflex activity (like peristalsis). Or one might be engaged in being merely active (like blinking, coughing, sweating, dozing, fainting, feeling annoyed, or contracting a fever).

In all such cases, one may be described as *active*, undoubtedly, but not as *exercising one's agency*. The point is that, though merely *active*, one is evidently still capable of picking oneself out of the perceptible environment in relation to other objects. So *SDT* is false.

We might take on a different definition:

(b) 'x is exercising its agency over the perceived environment just in case x is interacting with that environment'.[17]

'Interaction' is ambiguous as it occurs here.

A strong (i.e. reflexive) reading would claim that, if x interacts with y, then both must at least be exercising powers to make things happen over the other. But this is no help to the adversary: the problem of patient perceivers arises precisely because one side is not exercising such power over the other.

A weak (i.e. non-reflexive) reading would claim that x interacts with y just in case at least one exercises powers to make things

---

[16] Cf. Brewer (1992), p. 27.
[17] Cf. Brewer (1992), p. 26.

happen over the other. But then just being a *perceiver* would count as interacting with one's environment. And if interacting with one's environment counts as exercising agency over it, perceptual experience would be sufficient for perceptual self-location.

There is another difficulty with supposing the weak reading a plausible emendation. Suppose we accept that x is interactive given only that it is the object of some exercise of agency and that x is exercising its agency just in case it interacts with y. Then x will count as exercising its agency even if x has no power whatsoever to make anything happen. So much the worse for the emendation. (Note that there is of course no problem with supposing that y and x may interact and both exercise agency, for they may both have agency exercised on them – when oxygen rusts iron, it may be correct to say that oxygen acts on the metal and the metal acts on the oxygen).

Suppose, then, we adopt a third definition:

(c) 'x is exercising its agency over the perceived environment just in case x is engaging in purposive behaviour with respect to that environment'.[18]

Again, the phrase is ambiguous between strong and weak readings; and again, neither help the adversary.

Weak readings will allow that behaviour is purposive so long as it serves a purpose or goal. But then autonomic reflexes like blinking and peristalsis count as purposive behaviour, and so, of course, does perception. Consequently, perceptual experience alone would be sufficient for perceptually self-locating experience.

Strong readings will deny that being merely receptive to the perceptual flow counts as purposive behaviour with respect to the environment; they will require something like 'observable operations on that environment' from the candidate. But then the problem of patient perceivers is not answered. One may surely still have self-locating perceptions even if one chooses not to operate observably on the environment, or is restrained from so doing (Odysseus before the mast), or is incapable of so doing (the paralysed).

Third response

The opposite direction might be taken in responding to the problem of patient perceivers. Instead of claiming that the apparently

---

[18] Brewer (1992), p. 18.

perceptually self-locating subjects in these examples are in fact exercising their agency over the perceived environment, it might be claimed that their experience is *not* in fact perceptually self-locating. The response seems immediately implausible, but there are grounds to be examined.

i) *Elucidation.*

To suppose there could be perceptually self-locating experience in the absence of agency would leave the phenomenon high and dry, at least as regards its explanation.[19] This may be true. But, of course, it does not follow that one sees something desirable as being to one's left only if one would reach out in that direction. Consider the case of paralysed perceptual self-locators; they depend on others to exercise agency in this regard. We may even accept that the phenomenon of perceptual self-location requires explanation in terms of a general context of agency – i.e. there must *be* agents if the phenomenon is to serve a purpose. But *SDT* does not follow from this. For it does not entail that each perceptual self-locator be an agent.

ii) *The requirements on perceptual self-location.*

The point is sometimes attributed to Schopenhauer:

> the only adequate discrimination of the self as an element of the empirical world is anchored in one's interaction with the perceived environment.[20]

Now, to be perceptually self-locating, one must of course discriminate oneself from all other things. But there is apparently no reason to suppose that my examples involve people unable to do this. They may not be exercising their agency and nevertheless know both *what kind* of thing they are – given our assumption, they are right to think they are corporeal objects – and *which thing* they are, an awareness that may be given by perceiving one's solidity, shape, location, and spatio-temporal boundaries. Schopenhauer may be right that the phenomenon of self-discrimination is to be explained by appeal to interaction with the perceived environment. But this does not deliver *SDT* – both because interaction need not mean exercising one's agency, and

---

[19] As Cassam notes: 'A major part of the point of saying that someone sees something as being to her left rather than to her right is to explain why, if she desires the object, she would reach out in one direction rather than another' (1997), p. 84.

[20] Brewer (1992), p. 26.

because one need not actually be exercising one's agency to discriminate oneself.[21]

iii) *The dependence of perception on action.*

It has been said that

> A person incapable of voluntary self-movement cannot spontaneously generate the kind of motion parallax which ... is vital to extracting the spatial structure of his environment from the light energies encountered by his eyes.[22]

To support *SDT*, we have to assume that 'voluntary self-movement' entails the exercise of agency, and that motion parallax is vital to perceptual self-location. Both assumptions are plausible; the first obviously so, and the second because of undetermination considerations. Momentary viewings and hearings underdetermine the geometrical properties and relations of visible and audible objects in their spatial array. In motion, however, objects in one's environment are specified geometrically to a sufficiently high degree of accuracy.

But we may accept these claims without accepting *SDT*. For there are two gaps in the argument to be exploited. First, though parallax requires motion, it does not require motion in the *perceiver*; the movement of the objects perceived would be sufficient. Second, though the perceiver might move – thus generating the kind of parallax necessary for determined experience – the perceiver's movement does not require the exercise of their agency over the environment. Odysseus on his ship and the paralysed person on their moving hospital bed enjoy all that motion has to offer in respect of parallax. Since they are moved, they move without exercising their agency.

Thus we have no reason to deny that the experience of patient perceivers is perceptually self-locating. Similar points apply to keeping track of objects and monitoring them. Perceptual self-location undoubtedly depends on having these opportunities and abilities. But Odysseus can keep track both of the sirens and himself as he moves in relation to them, just as the paralysed person can, all without exercise of their agency.

So it seems to me that a problem of patient perceivers

---

[21] There are related points that will appear later in dealing with certain comments of Sydney Shoemaker.
[22] Lowe, *Subjects of experience* (Cambridge: CUP, 1996), p. 140.

remains for *SDT*; it suggests that the thesis is false – perception plus something less than agency is sufficient for egocentric spatial perception.

The insufficiency claim

We may turn now to the grounds for supposing that perceptual experience is insufficient for egocentric spatial perception, and to the general claim entailing this; namely the *Insufficiency Claim*, that perceptual experience is insufficient to provide for self-awareness of any sort.

Sydney Shoemaker is currently the foremost defender of this claim, though it is not always clear at precisely what strength. At one point, he summarises the aim of his discussion as 'denying that *self-awareness* involves *any* sort of perception of oneself'.[23] At another, however, he admits that 'there can occur something that is describable as "finding oneself in the world"' or 'being an object to oneself'; and he offers seeing oneself in a mirror as an example.[24] Shoemaker also claims that introspective self-awareness cannot count as perceptual awareness of oneself as a corporeal object.[25] I shall give reasons for rejecting both these claims.

Self-awareness and perception

Consider Shoemaker's claim that self-awareness involves no sort of perception of oneself. The position is apparently untenable – and not just because catching sight of oneself in the mirror may count as providing one with perceptual awareness of oneself. For this choice of example gives the false impression that the phenomenon occurs only intermittently and for visual perception alone. In fact, of course, the phenomenon occurs almost continuously for corporeal subjects and involves the use of all five senses. Thus looking at my hand typing this sentence, I am presented to myself 'as an object' in Shoemaker's sense – i.e. I see myself in just the way others are perceived by me as objects.

It is no objection that I cannot see *all* of myself in this way; for

---

[23] 'Self-Reference and Self-Awareness', reprinted in Q. Cassam (ed. 1994) *Self-Knowledge* (Oxford: Oxford University Press), p. 89; my emphases.

[24] (1968), p. 86.

[25] 'Introspection and the Self', reprinted in Q. Cassam (ed. 1994), pp. 118–39; 'Self-Knowledge and "Inner Sense"', reprinted in his *The First-Person Perspective and Other Essays*, (Cambridge: CUP, 1996), pp. 201–68.

I cannot see *all* of other corporeal subjects when presented with them either. As I speak, I am presented to myself as an audible object as others are to me. As Abelard washes himself in the bath, he also smells, tastes, and touches himself as an object – i.e. just as he might smell, taste, and touch others. These forms of perceptual self-awareness require an identification of the presented object as oneself. Consequently, we may legitimately be regarded as presented to ourselves in these ways 'as objects', thus fulfilling the conditions on perceptual self-awareness.

If it does make sense to talk of our routinely perceiving ourselves as corporeal objects, we have still to account for the fact that we are not always overly conscious of this. It may be that too conscious a perceptual awareness of ourselves would impede us – in performing actions, for example. This is one of the few occasions where the common sense of 'self-consciousness' (i.e. akin to anxiety, embarrassment) points up a moral about perceptual self-awareness. Consider a stock example: the potter who is unable to turn the clay if he concentrates on himself, the corporeal object making a pot, rather than on the pot itself. It may be for similar reasons that we are usually not reflectively aware of the sensations universally and routinely present in bodily awareness.

Bodily awareness can count as introspective self-awareness

Consider now Shoemaker's more specific claim: that introspective self-awareness cannot count as perceptual awareness of oneself as a corporeal object. I believe this claim is also false.[26] My argument against it can be broken down into several steps. In Shoemaker's own terms, bodily awareness can count as introspective self-awareness; as perceptual; and as of oneself as a corporeal object.

Consider, first, the claim that bodily awareness can count as introspective self-awareness.

Shoemaker's own definition of introspective awareness is that which serves as the basis for making first-personal statements in which *I* is used 'as subject' – i.e. statements that are immune to a certain kind of misidentification.[27] When I look in the mirror, I may know some thing to be F but be wrong about who is F – so

---

[26] I am indebted here to discussion of the relevant issues by Q. Cassam, 'Introspection and bodily self-ascription', in *The Body and the Self*, eds. Bermudez, Marcel and Eilan (MIT, 1995), pp. 311–336, and M. Martin, 'Bodily awareness' in the same volume, pp. 267–89. But I end up in a different place from either.

[27] (1986), pp. 119 ff.

this kind of awareness is not introspective: it does not ground first-personal statements that are immune to misidentification.

But there are kinds of bodily awareness that ground such statements – famously, those that ground most uses of 'my legs are crossed', 'my head aches', 'my back is bent', 'I am upside down', etc. Compare two situations in which I assert 'my fingers are pressing down on a table-top'. In the first case, say my fingers are numb and I am constrained to look only at a closed-circuit television screen. My assertion rests on my seeing a person I take to be me on this screen. Now I may know what *someone's* fingers are doing, but be wrong about whose they are – the figure I see is an actor made up to look like me. In the second case, my fingers are sensitive, I am not restrained, and my assertion rests on the various bodily sensations associated with tactile contact and pressure-exertion. It would make no sense to say 'someone's fingers are pressing down on a table-top, but is it me?' So the statement has that immunity to a particular kind of misidentification which makes the awareness on which it is based 'introspective'.

So bodily awareness can count as introspective.

Bodily awareness can count as perceptual

The second stage of my argument concerns the claim that bodily awareness can count as a kind of perception on Shoemaker's own account. Shoemaker offers various conditions 'satisfied by ordinary kinds of sense perception'.[28] And bodily awareness of the kinds that ground immunity statements also satisfies these conditions.

Consider the following scene: Abelard, who is in the bath, knows that someone is scratching his back and says 'I am scratching between my shoulder-blades'. Abelard knows it because he is alone in the bath and can feel his fingertips running up and down the length of a familiar scar. This example of bodily awareness fulfils Shoemaker's criteria for being introspective, for it serves as the basis for making first-personal statements that are immune to misidentification.[29] The question 'I know some particular thing is scratching between my shoulder-blades; but is it me?' would be quite redundant to Abelard. Moreover, this example of bodily awareness fulfils Shoemaker's eight conditions 'satisfied by ordinary kinds of sense perception'.

[28] (1996), p. 204.
[29] (1986), pp. 119 ff.

According to Shoemaker, sense perception must involve

the operation of an organ of perception whose disposition is to some extent under the voluntary control of the subject.[30]

Now the kind of bodily awareness Abelard is experiencing involves various receptors on his skin and below its surface, in his joints, internal organs and muscles over which he has the kind of control characteristic, for example, of vision. Just as it is not entirely up to us what we see when positioned in a certain way, even though we are relatively free in how we position ourselves, so Abelard is relatively free in what he does with his body (he is now touching his back; he could turn himself upside down; wholly immerse himself in water; etc), even though it is not entirely up to him how he perceives himself to be once engaged in whatever activity or posture he has taken up.

Sense perception, in Shoemaker's view, must also involve sense-experiences

that are distinct from the object of perception, and also distinct from the perceptual belief (if any) that is formed.[31]

Abelard might have felt his back to be a certain way, scarred for example, and yet have had no scar; and, knowing the illusion of old, though he cannot help feeling scarred, he would not then have believed that he was. And, more generally, bodily experiences are evidently belief-independent in the required sense. I may feel my leg to be a certain way and yet have no leg (no object of the experience); if I put my very-hot-hand into tepid water, I cannot help its feeling an icy-cold-hand to me, though I believe it is at worst by now a tepid-hand.

Shoemaker adds a further condition:

While sense perception provides one with awareness of facts, i.e. awareness *that* so and so is the case, it does this by means of awareness of objects.[32]

Abelard's awareness that there is pressure on his fingers and on his scar is explained by his awareness of the objects involved – his fingers, his back, their solidity, shape, location, impenetrability etc.

[30] (1996), pp. 204–5.
[31] (1996), p. 205.
[32] (1996), p. 205.

Shoemaker also holds that

> The perception of objects standardly involves perception of their intrinsic, nonrelational properties. To perceive that this book is to the right of that one I must perceive ... intrinsic properties of the two books, e.g. their colours and shapes.[33]

Perceiving the shape of this scar at his fingertips, without seeing it, by touch alone, involves Abelard's perceiving of the shape of his fingers and the hand to which they belong, information that is given through sensory-receptors in his fingers, their joints and in skin-stretch.

According to Shoemaker,

> Objects of perception are potential objects of attention.[34]

One's pressured finger is such an object. Without altering what one perceives, one can shift one's attention from it to the other fingers of one's hand which are lightly curled, compare them, and thereby enhance one's ability to gain differentiated knowledge about one's whole hand.

Shoemaker stipulates that

> Perceptual beliefs are causally produced by the objects or states of affairs perceived, via a causal mechanism that normally produces beliefs that are true.[35]

If this is true of perception in general, then there is no reason to deny that it is true of the kind of bodily awareness here described.

In Shoemaker's view,

> The objects and states of affairs which the perception is of, and which it provides knowledge about, exist independently of the perceiving of them, and, with certain exceptions, independently of there being things with the capacity for perceiving them or being aware of them.[36]

Since opponents explicitly allow that 'it is in principle possible for ... human bodies to exist in this way', this condition is fulfilled by bodily awareness.[37]

Finally, according to Shoemaker,

---

[33] (1996), p. 205.
[34] (1996), p. 206.
[35] (1996), p. 206.
[36] (1996), p. 206.
[37] (1996), p. 206.

> Sense perception affords 'identification-information' about the object of perception ... The provision of such information is involved in the 'tracking' of the object over time, and its reidentification from one time to another.[38]

So tracking an object requires perceptual information; it is difficult to see how this can be a condition on something's counting as perceptual awareness.

It would do if the passage were claiming that no awareness of an object, O, counts as perceptual awareness of that object unless the perceiver *does* use it to keep track of O. But this is untenable; we are continually being made perceptually aware of objects that we do not keep track of – because we cannot, need not, or choose not to.

The passage might mean that no awareness of an object, O, counts as perceptual awareness of that object unless the perceiver *could* use it to keep track of O if the need arose. But it is compatible with this interpretation to claim that awareness of oneself as subject is both perceptual and quite independent of keeping track. For suppose we think that no awareness could count as of the subject if it involves keeping track of the self.[39] Nevertheless it might be perceptual; it can hardly be counted against a form of awareness that it does not satisfy a need that could not arise.

Thus bodily awareness can count as both introspective and perceptual.

Introspective awareness can be of a corporeal object

The final step of the argument is to show that the kinds of bodily awareness that count as both introspective and perceptual may also count as offering awareness of oneself as a corporeal object.

Recall Abelard's report 'I'm scratching between my shoulder-blades'. The sensation on which his report is based is intrinsically located in his body as a spatio-temporally located, force-exerting, and impenetrably solid object. So, in having the sensation, he is aware of himself as a corporeal object. This is to draw attention to a point others have remarked on: as Brian O'Shaughnessy says

> the space and solidity of our bodies provides the access to the space and solidity of other bodies.[40]

---

[38] (1996), p. 205.
[39] Cassam notes and defends this interpretation of Shoemaker (1995), p. 329.
[40] *The Will: A Dual Aspect Theory* (Cambridge: Cambridge University Press 1989), p. 38.

For example, one might discover the solid and force-exerting properties of an object one is touching by recognising that one is not penetrating it – say as one presses one's fingers down on a table-top. And what gives us access to this information is the simultaneous awareness of one's body as an impenetrably solid and force-exerting object.

This claim might be vulnerable to attack if it were merely a matter of what Abelard learns through sensations. But the sense of touch cannot be reduced to a matter of using sensations of contact as a means of access to some perceived item. It is bodily awareness that is the basic means of access. After all, say his fingers are numb. Nevertheless, he would find that they, one part of his body, could not be moved through this object, which is another part. His awareness that this is the case is certainly not given through any sensation of contact, but rather through perceiving his body as a spatio-temporally located, force-exerting, and impenetrable item. That is, the body of which he is aware is experienced not only as subject (hence grounding first-personal statements that are immune to a certain kind of misidentification), but also as the bearer of properties whose possession by some item makes it a corporeal object.

A champion of *SDT* might suppose that we have here evidence for the thesis – the claim that perception plus something less than agency is insufficient for egocentric spatial perception. They might say, for example, that this introspective perceptual bodily awareness of a corporeal object is only available to one because one is exercising one's agency – pressing one's fingers on the table-top, for example. But this is clearly false. The example would have worked equally well if it were the table-top pressing on one's fingers – e.g. if it had fallen on top of one.

Consequently, using terms as Shoemaker has defined them, introspection can count as perceptual awareness of oneself as a corporeal object.

My overall purpose in this paper has been to understand how action and perception are related in self-awareness. The short-term goal has been to question the grounds and motivations for the overly-strong claim, *SDT*. This negative task is necessary before positive claims can be safely advanced. I have tried to meet the main arguments of the foremost supporters of the *Insufficiency*

Claim. My main positive claim has been that perceptual experience is sufficient to provide one with (introspective) self-awareness of oneself as a corporeal object.[41]

References

Banville, J. (2000). *Eclipse* (London: Picador).

Berkeley, G. (1710). *A Treatise concerning the principles of human knowledge* (Oxford: OUP, 1998).

Berkeley, G. (1713). *Three dialogues between Hylas and Philonous* (Oxford: OUP, 1998).

Brewer, B. (1992). 'Self-location and agency', *Mind*, 101, 17–34.

Campbell, J. (1994). *Past, Space and Self* (Cambridge: MIT Press).

Cassam, Q. (1995). 'Introspection and bodily self-ascription', in *The Body and the Self*, eds. Bermudez, Marcel and Eilan (MIT, 1995).

Cassam, Q. (1997). *Self and World* (Oxford: OUP, 1997).

Chisholm, R. (1994). 'On the observability of the self' in *Self-Knowledge*, ed. Q. Cassam (Oxford: OUP).

Davidson, D. (1980). *Essays on actions and events* (Oxford: OUP, 1980).

Hoffman, J. and Rosenkrantz, G. (1997). *Substance* (London: Routledge).

Hume, D. (1739). *A Treatise of Human Nature* (Oxford: OUP, 1978).

Hurley, S. (1998). *Consciousness in Action* (London: Harvard University Press).

Lowe, E.J. (1996). *Subjects of experience* (Cambridge: CUP, 1996).

Martin, M. (1995). 'Bodily awareness' in *The Body and the Self* eds. Bermudez, Marcel and Eilan (MIT, 1995).

Merleau-Ponty, M. (1945). *Phenomenology of Perception,* Translation: Colin Smith (London: Routledge, 1962).

O'Shaughnessy, B. (1989). *The Will: A Dual Aspect Theory* (Cambridge: Cambridge University Press).

Shoemaker, S. (1996). *The First-Person Perspective and Other Essays,* (Cambridge: CUP, 1996).

Strawson, P. (1959). *Individuals* (London: Methuen and Co.).

[41] I am most grateful to audiences at Pittsburgh, Oxford, Bremen and London (KCL) for discussion of arguments contained in this paper.

3

GENDER/BODY/MACHINE

Alison Adam

Introduction

far is a body, or embodiment, necessary for having knowledge and, crucially, how does this relate to gender? Are there types of AI which take embodiment into account in a meaningful way and are these better placed to enrol a concept of gender in their design?

Tackling these questions requires a consideration of the concept of the body in feminist theory. In particular, my concern is with embodiedness in feminist epistemology, where a central concern has been the role of the body in the making of knowledge, and how this may inform a critique of the artificial intelligence (AI) project and the related area of artificial life (A-Life), the latter area being of most interest in this paper. In constructing this critique, and by way of introduction, I wish to explore, more briefly, the tensions between the treatment of the body in different branches of feminist theory, especially the tensions between the approaches of feminist sociology and feminist philosophy. My intention is partly to dispel the idea that there is a unified approach to the problem of the body from feminist theory. Additionally I believe that some consideration of how to marry a sociological approach with a philosophical approach to the body is of more general interest, and the vehicle of feminist theory is appropriate for such a discussion, given that the body has proved to be such a dominant theme in feminist thinking. On route to this I explore the ways in which writing from category theory and anthropological phenomenology offers rich suggestions as to *how* the body has been left out of objectivist accounts of epistemology, but struggles to offer an account of *why*. In its analysis of the links between women, knowledge and the body, feminist revisions of epistemology offer a more convincing *why*. This is explored briefly through a critique of symbolic AI, and more substantially through the problem of embodiment in artificial life.

Feminism and the body

It is, perhaps, something of an understatement to say that there exists a tension in contemporary feminist writing on the body. Just as sociology, in general, and feminist philosophy too, have begun to take what Anne Witz (2000) has described as a 'corporeal turn', feminist sociology has, by contrast, moved away from the *materiality* of the body towards the *sociality* of women in sociological discourse. This tension mirrors many of my concerns with how the phenomenological body could connect with the body in society, with the manner in which these views of the body are connected to the production of knowledge and with the ways in which such an analysis may serve a critique of the project of AI and A-Life.

Much of the problem for feminist sociology lies in the dangers of naturalizing the body, particularly the female body, as therein lies the spectre of essentialism. Broadly speaking essentialism is the view that there are 'essential' or natural, fixed categories of masculinity and femininity that can be ascribed to men and women. Feminist sociology sees this as dangerous as the natural categories ascribed to woman usually circumscribe her inferiority. Hilary Rose (1994) reminds us of the dangers of sociobiology which has been used to naturalize social organization against a biological base and to disguise political positions which inevitably locate women in an inferior role. The trajectory of sociobiology is particularly pertinent as it signals the convergence of biology and computer science (Kember 2002). Life is digitized, genes are codes and the inevitability of certain forms of social organization is reinforced by their description in formalized, symbolic form.

Looking historically, such natural characteristics are often sharply presented. For instance, witness Victorian debates on women's lack of fitness for higher education on the grounds that it shrivels the reproductive organs or the push for women to return to the hearth after World War II when the supposed dangers of maternal deprivation were discovered. Tying gender to an allegedly uncontroversial factual definition of biological sex looks suspect and probably impossible for most feminists. This looks even more suspect when other supposedly uncontroversial aspects of male and female are attributed e.g. stereotypical notions that men are aggressive and women passive. Where do we draw the line? It is unlikely that a line can uncontrovertibly be drawn anywhere. Essentialism looms. Iris Young argues that forcing explanations of difference

onto a mysterious 'feminine essence' just makes difference inexplicable (1989: 142). On the one hand we must not deny real differences between the genders if they exist, but on the other we must
find realistic ways of rendering them intelligible. Elizabeth Grosz
(1994) argues that the sexually specific body is socially constructed
and that biology or nature is inherently social and has no pure or
natural core which can somehow stand outside culture. As the body
is the raw material of culture and society it is subject to endless
rewriting and reinscription. Sexual difference and the bodies on
which it is predicated are clearly volatile concepts.

Much of the concern of contemporary feminist sociology, and
indeed feminist philosophy, has revolved around the issue of the
cultural constitution of gender. But feminist sociology is left in a
difficult position in regard to the body. It needs to retain the
phenomenology of the body, whilst, at the same time, retaining its
conceptual grip of the complex, more than fleshly, grip on the
concept of gender. The problem here is that making the female
body too natural and too real, seems to load women with all sorts
of biological, and even, as suggested above, sociobiological baggage
of the 'biology as destiny' type. Second wave feminism has, understandably, expended much energy in its attempts to dispose of such
baggage. But at the same time, a retreat into unbridled postmodernism is problematic as the reality of embodied material oppression may be denied. Some of the tensions can be seen in reactions
to works such as Sara Ruddick's *Maternal Thinking: Towards a Politics
of Peace* (1989) which can be read as an important vector in the
development of contemporary feminist maternal ethics. Ruddick
argues that women have a special contribution to the ethics of care
derived from their experiences of motherhood and caring for children. However appealing the celebration of apparently feminine
characteristics might be for women, at the same time, the shackles
of an inevitable biology loom large. Can contemporary feminism
have it both ways? Can it chart a realistic course between the Scylla
of a relativist and potentially disembodied postmodernism and the
Charybdis of an essentialist biologism? The problem, as Witz
(2000) has noted, is to embody gender without overwhelming the
sociality of gender by corporeality.

Feminism and the body in the making of knowledge

Having considered some of the tensions which currently inhabit
feminist theory, particularly those existing between sociological

and philosophical approaches to the body, this section turns to the question of the role of the body in the making of knowledge, particularly as described in feminist epistemology, and how this can feed into a critique of representation of knowledge in artificial intelligence and artificial life.

Clearly feminist philosophy does not possess a monopoly over theories of corporeal aspects of knowledge. This is well-trodden ground in phenomenology and is, at least partly, encapsulated in Gilbert Ryle's (1963) elaboration of the 'propositional/skills' distinction. Two issues are important here. First of all, explanations for the underlying relationship of the body and the making of knowledge are often rendered less important than how the relationship operates. Feminist theory offers a number of important ways of thinking about explanations for that relationship which are not explored sufficiently in other bodies of theory. Secondly, it adds weight to feminist thought if feminist arguments are compatible with those of phenomenologists and category theorists who are similarly arguing against a rationalist or 'objectivist' metaphor, at the same time maintaining that the body plays a crucial role in the making of knowledge.

The work of George Lakoff (1987) and Mark Johnson (1987) (Lakoff and Johnson 1980: 1999), working on categories and prototypes, is especially useful in understanding the bodily basis of knowledge and rationality. Their work can be seen as part of a long running dialogue between philosophy and cognitive science whereby they promote the concept of the embodied mind through 'empirically responsible philosophy – a philosophy informed by an ongoing critical engagement with the best empirical science available' (Lakoff and Johnson 1999: 552). Their work is not informed by feminist theory, indeed Lakoff maintains a surprising degree of gender blindness to the connotations of one of his central examples, which revolves round the supposed 'dangerous' nature of women in some societies, in his *Women, Fire and Dangerous Things* (Lakoff 1987). This is all the more surprising given the way that gender appears to be one of the most fundamental categories we have for ordering and classifying our social worlds. Despite this, such a theoretical position may usefully be appropriated in the service of feminist epistemology.

For Lakoff, under the traditional view, reason is seen as abstract and disembodied.

On the new view, reason has a bodily basis. The traditional view sees reason as literal, as primarily about propositions that can be objectively either true or false. The new view takes imaginative aspects of reason – metaphor, metonymy, and mental imagery – as central to reason, rather than as a peripheral and inconsequential adjunct to the literal (Lakoff 1987: xi).

Lakoff finds evidence for his view of experiential realism in the way people categorize the natural world, a study of which he develops in the domain of prototype theory. In a similar vein, the work of Eleanor Rosch (1973) is also influential, in language and linguistic categories and metonymy i.e. where a subcategory has a socially recognized status as standing for the category as a whole. An instance of this is the housewife-mother category, where the category 'working mother' is defined in contrast to the stereotypical 'housewife-mother', even though a very substantial number of mothers with children of school age or younger may actually have paid employment. Lakoff acknowledges that such categories are cultural conventions and they fulfil a normative role. The 'mother' example clearly demonstrates a cultural imperative of homemaker-as-norm, no matter what the reality of the level of mothers' participation in the workforce might be. Unfortunately Lakoff is unaware of the way that this example also serves to reinforce the low esteem in which societies hold the work of women who stay at home to the extent that their work is not even regarded as work at all.

Lakoff argues strongly for the relationship between the body and the formation of mental concepts. The objectivist account of cognition, meaning and rationality makes no mention of who or what is doing the thinking; the implication is that it does not matter. The function of the human organism is deemed irrelevant, and thought is characterized as symbol manipulation, where the symbols are taken to have a fixed correspondence with things and categories in the world. Such a view has been directly transported into the design of classical AI systems. The notion of a fixed correspondence echoes Daniel Dennett's (1993) concerns with the way that AI fails to ground the semantics of symbols to something in the world. For instance, there is apparently nothing to connect a daffodil with the symbol for a daffodil. And this also strikes a chord with the 'view from nowhere' of traditional epistemology which Thomas Nagel (1986) has described – in other words an epistemology that presumes that the identity of the knower is unimportant and need not be identified, that the same knowledge is universally available. Unsurprisingly the 'view from nowhere' has been subject to much criticism from feminist epistemologists who argue strongly for the situated nature of knowledge (Code 1993).

The objectivist account suggests that concepts are just there in the world for us to perceive through the senses, and the body has no role in adding to the meaning of concepts. Under Lakoff's view, experientialist semantics must go beyond mere symbol manipulation as the embodiment of concepts is made directly, through perception, and indirectly through knowledge embodied in social groups.

The independence of metaphysics and epistemology is the lynchpin of objectivism which is epitomised in Quine's, 'To be is to be the value of a variable'. Yet such a view is completely contradicted by studies in cultural anthropology (ibid.: 208). It is as if mathematical logic is being asked to do too much work, especially in linguistics and in AI, where it is presumed to be a universal language which can express everything that is important for everyone, hence it can be seen as doing a job for which it was never originally designed. So really Lakoff and Johnson's 'objectivism' is a more general term which includes, in its purview, traditional epistemology and its manifestation in symbolic AI. Their attack is based, in particular, on the way that the role of the body has been ignored in objectivist or logicist accounts.

In contrast, the experientialist approach of Lakoff and Johnson attempts to characterize meaning in terms of the nature and experience of the organism doing the thinking. Meaning is seen in terms of *embodiment*; '. . . meaning is understood via real experiences in a very real world with very real bodies. In objectivist accounts, such experiences are simply absent' (ibid.: 206).

Categorization theory gives convincing explanations of *how* the body is ignored in the production of knowledge. But, importantly, it falls short of a broader explanation of *why* the body should have been excluded so effectively from the making of knowledge in the first place. It seems to have forgotten one of the most fundamental categories of all, namely gender. This is an important job for feminist theories of epistemology. In order to do this, I now want to explore the ways in which the concept of the material body has often been linked more specifically to women rather than to men and what this tells about why the body is excluded from traditional accounts of epistemology.

As I have already described, the body has become increasingly important in feminist theory, even if there is no consensus as to how it should be treated. The way that feminist epistemology understands the role of the body in the production of knowledge, is especially of interest for the present discussion. For instance, Nancy Goldberger argues for the role of a 'gut' or visceral knowing in her empirical studies of women's knowledge (1996: 352). Much of this work aspires to be a refutation of essentialism as feminists have understandably been wary of views of the body which tie it too closely to nature and reproduction (Grosz 1991: 1). Yet at the same time many of the traditional philosophies most closely allied to feminism, such as Marxism and socialism, have a tendency to subordinate the body and to transcend it. Feminist theory argues that this is no accident; such a move forms the *leitmotiv* of Western rationalist philosophy.

Hence philosophies of liberation and antiobjectivism, which might have formed feminist theory's natural allies, hold a deep seated view of the triumph of reason over nature. For feminism, the tension lies between an avoidance of biologism and essentialism, whilst at the same time seeing the female body as 'a preeminently sociocultural artifact or construct' (ibid.: 2). As Kirby claims, the debate between essentialism and antiessentialism encourages 'somatophobia' (1991: 4). I would also suggest that a similar somatophobia lies at the heart of the cognitive 'information processing' or symbolic approach to AI, and indeed is present at least in screen-based forms of A-Life. Both of these can be seen, in some sense, as contemporary, computational strains of Cartesian philosophy, which splits off and elevates the mind over the body.

The division of reason and nature is a prominent theme in much feminist writing (Diprose 1994, Gatens 1996, Grosz 1993, Harding 1991, Hein 1992, Rose 1994). This writing looks at women's lives to see that women are assigned the work that men apparently do not want to do. Women's lives and experiences are to do with bodies, the bearing and raising of children, the looking after of bodies, the young, old and sick and men's bodies too.

There are some interesting ways in which this can be illustrated. If one thinks of Mary Douglas's work (1966) on boundaries and their maintenance in the social order, that which crosses a boundary may pollute. One such pollution we define as dirt, 'matter out of place.' There are gender relations even in dirt. This point struck me during a talk on the UK Engineering Council's WISE (Women into Science and Engineering) campaign which I attended some years ago.[1] One of WISE's roles is to persuade women and girls to enter the engineering profession where they are currently underrepresented. The speaker suggested that women should not mind that engineering is 'dirty' – one thinks of machine oil under the fingernails here – because women are used to cleaning up dirt. However professional engineers do not usually get dirty anyway – they work in offices which are cleaned at night or early in the morning by an invisible army of working class women. So class as well as gender is implicated in dirt. But allowing for the moment that engineers deal with dirt, I contend that it is a different sort of dirt to that which women must clean up, because women deal with biological dirt, created by and emanating from bodies, not machines, which belong to the world of men.

Women belong to the location of bodies in domestic work in their own, and others' homes, and in the workplace. Harding (1991) describes this as concrete work (it is also described similarly by Suchman (1994) as a form of articulation work) – the better women are at it the more invisible it becomes. In fact the invisibility of such labour has become institutionalized in many systems of thought – one looks in vain in Marx's Capital for a discussion of *housework*. Indeed, even a newer theory of economics, specifically designed to included the hitherto neglected area of home economics, that of Nobel prize winning Becker, *still* neglects women's central role in domestic economy, by assuming that the family has an altruistic male head, that the family acts to maximize total utility and that women are best served by the protection of marriage (Cudd 2001).

Women's traditional work is then often rendered invisible, certainly from a professional male perspective – feminists argue that it frees men in the ruling groups to immerse themselves in the life of the mind – the world of abstract concepts, while caring for bodies and the places that they exist disappears into 'nature', in a process which Hilary Rose describes as, women's 'compulsory altruism'(1994, p. 40). This type of bodily, concrete yet invisible labour produces a type of knowledge which is regarded as subordinate to mental knowledge, if it is regarded as knowledge at all. Small wonder then that the machines that AI gives birth to are mental machines devoid of bodies and bodily knowledge.

---

[1] Women into Computing Conference, De Montfort University, June 1997.

Woman's identity has traditionally been associated with the body and nature, just as man's has been located in their transcendence as mind and culture. Woman is thereby positioned as man's attenuated inversion, as mere specular reflection through which his identity is grounded. The brute matter of woman's embodiment and the immediacy of her lived experience provide the corporeal substratum upon which man erects himself and from which he keeps a safe distance (Kirby 1991: 5).

This split rests on the ancient dichotomy of spirit and matter. Hilde Hein (1992) suggests that the Aristotelian/Christian tradition opposed matter and spirit and attributed them, respectively, to the female and male principles. Spirit was associated with the rational, principled and ethically sound and was superior to dark, passive matter, a nature to be dominated and controlled. Such a position found voice in the Baconian view of science's domination over nature, and gives us the *man of reason*, the ideal of rationality associated with the rationalist philosophies of the seventeenth century (Lloyd 1984). The *man of reason* strengthens the associations between 'male' and 'rational' and between 'female' and 'non-rational'. The Cartesian method of the seventeenth century further reinforces distinctions between mind and matter, emphasizing clear and distinct reasoning and eliminating emotions and sensuality. Susan Bordo argues that social manipulation of the female body has been a central plank in maintaining power relations between the sexes for at least the past hundred years (1993: 143). Following Foucault she reminds us that, although the logic of the power relations may be historically visible that does not mean that someone has planned it that way; we must not imply a conspiracy of men over women.

So what is feminism to make of the body now? There is obviously a danger here. In order to avoid essentialism we may end up disembodying the body – making it into something purely cultural and letting gender float free. Yet this shores up the view to be found in social constructivism, a view which can be read as androcentric, in that everything must been seen in terms of its cultural use (Bigwood 1991: 59). Feminists of a realist persuasion (e.g. Rose 1994, Harding 1991), and philosophers and cognitive scientists of a phenomenological cast (e.g. Dreyfus 1996, Johnson 1987, Lakoff 1987), *do* wish to retain a measure of realism, so that the embodied body may be retained in the face of the relativism which social constructivism seems to promise. An unfettered postmodernism is also problematic as it effectively disembodies the body, partly by its tendency to reduce everything to text, but also by its unwillingness to privilege one 'story' over another, thus making it difficult to construct material claims.

How can feminism naturalize the body whilst steering clear of the twin problems of essentialism and a disembodied postmodernism? And, importantly, can we include arguments from feminist epistemology, particularly in the shape of Vrinda Dalmiya and Linda Alcoff's (1993) research which shows a strong link between skills knowledge, gender-experiential knowledge and the body? The question of *embodiment* both for feminist theory, phenomenology and anthropological category theory rests on the role of the body in producing knowledge. What, then, does this say for the project of symbolic AI?

In the wake of history's elevation of pure reason as the Cartesian ideal, it is no surprise that propositional knowledge has found a voice as the pinnacle of true knowledge, and indeed no surprise that large and prestigious projects in artificial intelligence are based on such a Cartesian view of reason. A particularly good example of such a project is the Cyc project (Lenat and Guha 1990). Cyc was originally intended to act as an expert system to provide consensual knowledge, the background knowledge that one would need to understand a one volume encyclopaedia. Its basic design involved thousands of rules containing propositions relating to common sense such as: 'If my left foot is France, my right foot is in France.' However even if we *can* express such things propositionally, this is not how we know about the positioning of our feet. Were I to stand on the England/Scotland border with my feet apart you would understand exactly my little game. However Cyc would need to be told that there are special circumstances in which one's two feet may be in different countries. Hubert Dreyfus (1992) has criticized this project and expects it to fail. However it can be argued that success or failure might best be seen in cultural rather than philosophical terms, having attracted huge amounts of industry support and employing upwards of eighty people for fifteen or so years (a person millennium of effort no less!) we must conclude that the project has, at least in some terms, been a success even though it does not do what it set out to do. Dreyfus's critique of Cyc rests on its inability to represent anything but propositional knowledge. Crucially, skills type knowledge, as it depends on having a body, cannot usually be represented in propositional form. In concurring with those arguments generally, I want to add the missing gender dimension. I contend that a focus on propositional knowledge invalidates the lived experience of women's work and renders invisible the skilled bodily knowledge which that brings. However the argument cannot rest here. It is not purely a question of ignoring some aspects of knowledge; it is the question of whether these ways of knowing are crucial to having propositional knowledge itself; it is a question of whether these ways of knowing are essential to knowing anything at all.

AI and A-Life

In summary, my concern with the representation of knowledge in traditional symbolic AI is that, as women's ways of knowing have traditionally been based on the body, these are left out in much the same way that traditional AI leaves out the skills part of our knowledge. Feminist epistemology and related theory explains something of why that comes about in the elevation of the mind over the body and how these are related to masculine and feminine.

But it is important to consider whether the criticisms I level at symbolic AI can apply to other forms of AI. When we talk of symbolic AI we mean a computer system where the knowledge is all represented symbolically; one might have in mind something like a rule-based expert system. But the connectionist or neural network paradigm has long been hailed as a radical alternative to the symbolic approach. However I believe that for the purposes of my argument connectionist systems are not qualitatively different from symbolic systems. At bottom, they are no more physically or culturally situated than their symbolic sisters.

However the newer area of artificial life or 'A-Life' may offer an interesting alternative. Such A-Life systems can be screen based systems, modelling populations of simple individuals or can be robots often designated evolutionary robots, mobile robots or mobots. A-life is strongly informed by a 'selfish gene' style computational biology which draws much inspiration from sociobiology. Indeed I have described it elsewhere as 'sociobiology in computational clothing' (Adam 1998: 150). This is the most problematic aspect of such research for feminist theories.

A-Life, including both robotics and screen-based simulations, locates itself as a special kind of theoretical biology. In subscribing to a computational view of evolution, it is not surprising to discover that the biological models which A-Life draws from are heavily indebted to sociobiology. This section explores the appeal of sociobiology for A-Lifers and what this means for feminist theory. Once more, this concerns the body and the epistemological implications of bodily ways of knowing, especially in relation to considerations of gender.

Sociobiology rose to prominence in the 1970s and early 1980s through the works of Richard Dawkins (1976) and Edward Wilson (1975) amongst others. It can be characterized as a form of biological determinism where the social behaviour of individuals is to be explained by their biology and, in particular, by the preservation and continuance of individuals' genes, to the extent that Dawkins can claim this as 'the ultimate rationale for our existence' (quoted in Haraway 1991: 43). For Dawkins (1989), it is genes alone that are handed on from one generation to another, and it is pedantic to argue otherwise. He does not appear to see the transference of culture as on a par with genetics in determining what we pass from one generation to another. He is clearly interested in the possibilities afforded by A-Life, and has been associated with the programme, at least in its early stages, as he has himself created a biomorph computer program of his *Blind Watchmaker* in the mid-1980s (1986; 1991).

Hilary Rose (1994) sees the relationship between sociobiology and the new right as a love match. It was seized upon in the USA to fuel the arguments of IQ advocates in the discussion surrounding race and class, to justify cutting welfare benefits to poor, often black, women and their children. In the UK, it fitted the ideology of early Thatcherite Britain to keep women in the home and out of the labour market, although these arguments changed somewhat later in the 1980s to suit women, representing cheap labour, returning to the workforce in poorly paid part time work under the guise of 'flexible working'. These were the old 'biology as destiny' arguments dressed up in a shiny new sociobiology, to legitimate white male domination over female and black subordination, seen as rooted in biology, and therefore natural. When sociobiology is used to buttress many unpleasant aspects of stereotypical male behaviour, such as promiscuity and rape, it is unsurprising that the mid-1980s saw a concerted backlash from feminists. As Rose (ibid.) describes it, this was an attempt, by feminists, to move the debate about women from nature to culture. This can be seen against the backdrop of the radical science movement of that period, also related to the growth of social constructivist approaches to science, which had by then begun to undermine the claims to objectivity of the natural sciences, in exposing their socially constructed nature as part and parcel of our cultures (Knorr-Cetina 1981). But we should also be aware that some of the backcloth of this debate has been played out in the so-called 'science wars.' Briefly, at least for the scientists involved, the objectivity of science is at stake once again (Ashman and Barringer 2001). It is a debate which has resurfaced; one parent is the old 'two cultures' debate, but the other parent derives from internal/external debates in the history and philosophy of science in the 1970s and 1980s. With these aged parents, we could be forgiven for thinking that the science wars have a distinctly old-fashioned feel to them. Whereas its parents did not engage with feminism, partly because feminist theory was much less developed then and therefore did not mount a substantial challenge, the current science wars definitely do engage, particularly with feminist epistemologies of science as exemplified in Sandra Harding's (1991) work.

To return to the problematic nature of sociobiology, if feminists should be suspicious of the ideological uses of sociobiology, in maintaining traditional views of race class, gender and IQ, they must also be aware of the way in which the language of sociobiology designates itself as a part of information theory, in ways which parallel cognitive science's view of the behaviour of the mind as a symbol processor. Donna Haraway claims that sociobiology is the science of capitalist reproduction (1991: 44–45). Prewar biology was couched in terms of the clinical and medical; post-war sociobiology takes the language of the engineering science of automated technical devices, understood in terms of cybernetic systems. Organic form gives way to systems theory where the human body almost becomes an outmoded symbol-using device. Biology is transformed from a science of sexual organisms to one of reproducing genetic assemblages. The language is that of the machine and the market. Sociobiology studies societies in terms of zones of communication and exchanges of information. Our genes instruct us; we are behaving machines.

> . . . sociobiological reasoning applied to human sciences easily glides into facile naturalization of job segregation, dominance hierarchies, racial chauvinism, and the 'necessity' of domination

in sexually based societies to control the nastier aspects of genetic competition (ibid.: 67).

It is easy to see why sociobiology has the credentials to be the language of A-Life as it offers a view of biology in computer terms; one might almost say a view of biology almost waiting to be implemented. Indeed Chris Langton's (1989) early description of the field is couched in exactly the descriptions of phenotype, genotype and the overriding importance of the gene, favoured by the sociobiologists

But even if A-Life is sociobiology in computer clothing, must it carry with it the deterministic aspects of the parent discipline so disliked by feminists? In a sense there is a 'weak A-Life', which is analogous to John Searle's (1987) 'weak AI'. Weak A-Life can be characterized as the view that A-Life simulations offer the potential to show us interesting things about the way life has evolved, and could evolve in terms of say, bi-lateral symmetry, bodily segmentation and so on. On the other hand, 'strong A-Life' would be the view that we were actually creating life in these simulations, or that we were accurately representing all the important things about life in the growth of populations.

Dawkins' own exploration of A-Life is an eminent example of the weak version, as he sees the use of artificial life, 'not as a formal model of real life but as a generator of insight into our understanding of real life' (Dawkins 1989: 201). Yet this does not appear to be the view of many A-Lifers who appear to claim something stronger for their discipline. Such a view is put forward by Stefan Helmreich (1994), an anthropologist whose field work in the Sante Fe Institute for the Sciences of Complexity, one of the USA's most important A-Life labs, represents a sophisticated piece of research into the culture of A-Lifers. The strongly deterministic, aggressively individualistic worlds mirrored in A-Life simulations are sociobiology writ large in *silico* and as I shall suggest below, feminists should rightly be suspicious.

Embodiment and A-Life

Helmreich (ibid.) claims that A-Life promises not just the employment of biological notions in simulations to make machines more natural or life-like. Computational metaphors are applied to understanding nature to the extent that A-Lifers claim that life is a property of the formal *organization* of matter, and not just of matter itself. It is interesting to note that this is a modern form of a very old idea. It is very close to the arguments of some nineteenth century scientific materialists for a belief in the spontaneous generation of micro-organisms and the nature of *vital force* (Adam 1989). Emergent A-Life can, therefore, be seen as a form of computational spontaneous generation. Helmreich explains that this makes sense of the attempt to create life *in silico*. Reproduction is reduced to the passing of genetic *information* from one generation to another making it easy to replicate such processes by machine.

His study points to a number of revealing elements involved in the importation of cultural metaphors in the work of A-Lifers. Firstly there is the notion of 'playing god' in the creation stories of the artificial A-Life worlds, where a masculine god, or rather an active male programmer, breathes life into a female program. For instance the evolutionary biologists hold to a rhetoric of a 'hands-off' approach in letting their robot control mechanisms evolve, but it is they, not some natural environment, who interfere to set the tasks which the robots must evolve their control systems to achieve. It is like Newton's view of a god who only interferes to 'wind up' the solar system when it threatens to run down. Secondly there is the wish of the largely male scientists to create their own computational offspring, where, in A-Life simulations, parentage is to be defined as an informational relation rather than anything else (Helmreich 1994: 10).

What the A-Lifers choose to model in their artificial world is interesting, because it mirrors the view of Sandra Harding (1991) and Hilary Rose (1994) that women's labour in looking after bodies and bodily needs is invisible, and therefore to many men, trivial. Here is another example of a type of knowledge associated with women and bodies which is unacknowledged and therefore unrepresented in formal systems. Surely only a social group unaware of the labour involved in maintaining bodies and their needs could take such a view of the 'disembodied' nature of the important things in life. Helmreich paints a vivid picture of life at the Santa Fe Institute (ibid.: 13). Toilet paper is magically replenished, offices are cleaned, food is served. 'When researchers return sated from 3:30 tea and cookies to gaze at their computational worlds of simulated life, they can leave their bodies behind, in the true hacker tradition. They can sit there for hours on end lost in the computer'.

Significantly, such a masculine view of the important things in life finds a voice in the processes which are simulated in artificial worlds. Even in the robotic worlds of mobots and evolutionary robots, the robots' tasks involve wandering about; at best they are given tasks such as removing drinks cans. They do not mimic the more persuasive evolutionary behaviour of searching for food, shelter and looking after their young. I have yet to hear of a robot dying of starvation, hypothermia or a broken heart. They are mapped out in behaviourist terms, yet with a limited behavioural repertoire, one which hardly reflects suitable evolutionary characteristics and one which does not acknowledge gender differences in knowledge or work.

The Echo system

John Holland's Echo system contains strings of alphabetic characters which are manipulated by a lengthy C program that runs the Echo 'universe' (Holland 1993a, 1993b; Holland and Langton 1992). The strings are modelled as the genomes of agents that interact in an environment of renewable resources. The three categories of interaction of the A-Life agents in Echo are 'combat', 'trade' and 'mating'. Echo agents roam around their virtual environment, consuming resources, paying taxes and, somewhat responsibly, mating only if they have above a certain threshold of personal resource. Agents with zero length genomes which could reproduce without any resources (and therefore who paid no tax), were coded out of the system. Echo is a world of genetic determinism and ruthless competitive individualism. Only those who see themselves as self-determining individuals ignoring the invisible labour of others could develop such a model which leaves out so many things; the labour involved in looking after children, in looking after the domestic sphere, preparing and cooking meals, cleaning homes. Is nobody in the Echo world playing instead of working, mating or fighting? Where are the gays and lesbians in this society, the single parents on social benefits, the sick, old and disabled whom we care for because we believe that it is right in a civilised society? Apparently they are to be programmed out of the system in a kind of artificial eugenics.

Although robotic A-Life is heavily tied to embodiment, it is hard to escape from the argument that screen-based A-Life simulations ignore the problem of embodiment simply because the designers of such systems are so unaware of the invisible labour which keeps their own bodies functioning, keeps the spaces where their bodies exist functioning and importantly cares for their children.

Some of the sociobiological elements of A-Life are even more problematic and it can be demonstrated that arguments based on sociobiology could be reinforced and bolstered by their A-Life counterparts. Echo's zero-resource genomes were removed from the system as the programmers suggested that the program would quickly consume all available memory and grind to a halt anyway. This mirrors political concerns about consumption; witness the continuing backlash from the right of British politics against single mothers who are seen to consume, in living off state benefits, paying no taxes, in an extraordinary political system which forces many single mothers to stay on benefit rather than becoming economically active. This happens partly because of the high cost of unsubsidized childcare, and partly because any work earnings immediately reduce benefits by the same amount, meaning that they are, in effect, working for nothing. Are these Echo's zero resource genomes and will they be written out of the system?

Thinking now more specifically about robots, the evolutionary style of robotics also plays host to a view of nature red in tooth and claw. Evolutionary robots do not even mate, trade or indulge in combat – there is little fun in their lives.[2] 'Successful' robot control systems can contribute genetic material to become 'parents', which reduces parenthood or at least fitness for parenthood to ability to perform tracking and homing tasks (Wheeler 1996: 218). Robot control systems who are not very good at these tasks are 'discarded', and will not contribute genetically to successive generations. Both in the screen-based and in the robotics versions of A-Life there is an artificial eugenics at work which either prevents from becoming a parent, or actually deletes, those who are viewed to be not contributing to society in the appropriate way i.e. in the ways decided by the designers of the systems. A-Life societies are not

---

[2] However, a recent virtual visit to the humanoid robots project in MIT's AI laboratory reveals a lovely picture of the famous Cog robot playing with a slinky! http://www.mit.edu/

liberal democracies where individual members may reproduce if they so choose, regardless of their economic status or their abilities to perform some rather constrained tasks involving moving about in their environment. And who is choosing the deletions? – not the programs themselves as in an evolutionary world, but the programmers tinkering and playing god in the artificial world.

In terms of embodiment, situated and evolutionary based robotics, such as the MIT Cog project, provide clear alternatives to symbolic AI. They are also qualitatively different from screen based A-Life which seems little better than traditional AI in respect of bodily skills. Mobotics and evolutionary robotics represent a very real attempt to get away from the problems that bedevil symbolic AI, where at least some level of skilled, experiential, bodily knowledge is represented, e.g. the skill to avoid objects whilst moving around, the skill to pick up cups without breaking them or spilling the liquid inside – some of the skills, at any rate, which we learned as babies. Yet there are two problems with the sense of situatedness which they display. First of all the other sense of situatedness – social and cultural situatedness – is, as yet, absent. Some, but not all of this, is related to the ways in which their physical behaviour is, as yet, so limited. The work of feminist writers, including Lorraine Code (1993) on epistemic communities and Annette Baier (1985) on second person knowing, points to this aspect as being crucial to our knowledge of the world. As Cog is a robot baby, we can only speculate as to what kind of childhood Cog will have, and if the builders of Cog want to make it more socially situated how they will achieve it. It is not clear whether Cog needs a gender. The first thing we are told about a baby after it is born is whether it is a boy or a girl. Indeed it is very interesting to note that on the Cog FAQ web page, one of the first questions is 'does Cog have a gender?' to which the answer is 'No, Cog is an "it".' One wonders why people ask this; it obviously matters. Similarly one wonders why Cog's designers will not give it a gender.

If, as I suggest, bodily ways of knowing are left out of much of the AI project, we should also acknowledge how this impacts on cultural ways of knowing. As Bordo (1989) following Bourdieu, points out, the body is the means of transmission of much cultural knowledge e.g. table manners, toilet manners etc. '. . . the docile, regulated body practiced at and habituated to the rules of cultural life' (Bordo 1989: 13).

Conclusion

More of a concern with social and cultural situatedness would also militate against the cruder forms of biological determinism in A-Life's sociobiological models. Although the robots are embodied, they are embodied in a sense which ignores feminine aspects of embodiment, crucially the aspect of caring for bodies. Parenthood could be seen in terms of ability to care for and bring up children, with all the attendant open-ended knowledge that this brings of how to get babies to sleep and how to handle children and so on, rather than the ability to conform to a constrained economic or task based model. We could have robots falling in love and caring for, feeding, protecting and teaching baby robots rather than spending their time searching for empty drinks cans or trying to find the centre of a room. This then further emphasizes, something which child psychologists have known for years, that you need to go through the stages of childhood to become a well-rounded adult. Leaving technicalities aside, it seems unlikely that we could build a person; it is more realistic to grow one.

Much of the moderation exercised by symbolic AI after its own boom and bust years has been forgotten in the excitement of the new A-Life and surrounding virtual reality technologies. It is hard to escape the conviction that, once again, there is rationalist epistemology again writ large, but now with a strong theme of sociobiology. A-Life can ignore important bodily ways of knowing, drawn from the labour of women in looking after bodies, in its models. A-Life models purport to model whole societies, yet in a way that often emphasizes the worst part of societies. There is little room for passion, love and emotion in the knowledge created in A-Life worlds. A-Life's attachment to sociobiological models is based on an essentialist view of human nature and women's nature; where cultural ways of knowing are to be explained and subsumed in deterministic biological models. All this must be seen against the backcloth of the feminist movement's hard won battles to distance itself from 'biology as destiny' arguments.

In conclusion, a feminist epistemological critique of AI and A-Life technologies apparently paints a gloomy picture of omissions. But this need not be so. The more we understand the role of the body in the making of knowledge, the more we attend to the role of gender and other cultural variables, the richer will be our designs for these intelligent artefacts, and the possibility for useful and liberatory technology is opened up.

References

Adam, A. (1989). *Spontaneous Generation in the 1870s: Victorian Scientific Naturalism and its Relationship to Medicine* (unpublished Ph.D. thesis, Sheffield City Polytechnic, UK).

Adam, A. (1998). *Artificial Knowing: Gender and the Thinking Machine* (London and New York: Routledge).

Ashman, K. and Baringer, P. (eds) (2001). *After the Science Wars*, (London and New York: Routledge).

Baier, A. (1985). *Postures of the Mind: Essays on Mind and Morals* (Minneapolis, Minn.: University of Minnesota Press).

Bigwood, C. (1991). 'Renaturalizing the body (with the help of Merleau-Ponty)', *Hypatia*, 6, pp. 54–73.

Bordo, S. (1989). 'The body and the reproduction of femininity: a feminist appropriation of Foucault', in A. Jaggar and S. Bordo (eds) *Gender/Body/Knowledge: Feminist Reconstructions of Being and Knowing* (New Brunswick NJ: Rutgers University Press), pp. 13–33.

Bordo, S. (1993). *Unbearable Weight: Feminism, Western Culture, and the Body* (Berkeley, Los Angeles and London: University of California Press).

Code, L. (1993). 'Taking subjectivity into account', in L. Alcoff and E. Potter (eds) *Feminist Epistemologies* (New York and London: Routledge), pp. 15–48.

Cudd, A. (2001). 'Objectivity and ethno-feminist critiques of science', in K. Ashman and P. Baringer (eds) *After the Science Wars* (London and New York: Routledge), pp. 80–97.

Dalmiya, V. and Alcoff, L. (1993). 'Are "Old Wives' Tales" justified?', in L. Alcoff and E. Potter (eds) *Feminist Epistemologies* (New York and London: Routledge), pp. 217–244.

Dawkins, R. (1976). *The Selfish Gene* (Oxford: Oxford University Press).

Dawkins, R. (1986). *The Blind Watchmaker* (Harlow, UK: Longman).

Dawkins, R. (1989). 'The evolution of evolvability', in C. Langton (ed.) *Artificial Life, SFI Studies in the Sciences of Complexity* (Redwood, Cal.: Addison-Wesley), pp. 201–220.

Dawkins, R. (1991). *Blind Watchmaker: The Program of the Book* (P.O. Box 59, Leamington Spa: SPA).

Dennett, D. (1993). 'Allen Newell, Unified Theories of Cognition', *Artificial Intelligence* 59, pp. 285–294.

Diprose, R. (1994). *The Bodies of Women: Ethics, Embodiment and Sexual Difference* (London and New York: Routledge).

Douglas, M. (1966). *Purity and Danger: An Analysis of the Concepts of Pollution and Taboo* (London and New York: Ark).

Dreyfus, H. (1992). *What Computers Still Can't Do: A Critique of Artificial Reason* (Cambridge, Mass. and London: MIT Press).

Dreyfus, H. (1996). 'Response to my critics,' *Artificial Intelligence* 80, pp. 171–191.

Gatens, M. (1996). *Imaginary Bodies: Ethics, Power and Corporeality* (London and New York: Routledge).

Goldberger, N. (1996). 'Cultural imperatives and diversity in ways of knowing', in N. Goldberger, J. Tarule, B. Clinchy and M. Belenky (eds) *Knowledge, Difference and Power: Essays Inspired by Women' Ways of Knowing* (New York: BasicBooks/HarperCollins), pp. 335–71.

Grosz, E. (1991). 'Introduction to Hypatia special issue on the body', *Hypatia* 6, pp. 1–3.

Grosz, E. (1994). *Volatile Bodies: Toward a Corporeal Feminism* (Bloomington and Indianapolis: Indian University Press).

Haraway, D. (1991). *Simians, Cyborgs and Women: The Reinvention of Nature* (London: Free Association Books).

Harding, S. (1991). *Whose Science? Whose Knowledge?: Thinking from Women's Lives* (Milton Keynes: Open University Press).

Hein, H. (1992). 'Liberating philosophy: an end to the dichotomy of spirit and matter', in A. Garry and M. Pearsall (eds) *Women, Knowledge and Reality: Explorations in Feminist Philosophy* (New York and London: Routledge), pp. 293–311.

Helmreich, S. (1994). 'Anthropology inside and outside the looking-glass worlds of artificial life', unpublished paper, Department of Anthropology, Stanford University, Stanford, Cal. (Available from author at this address or by email on stefang@leland.stanford.edu).

Holland, J. (1993a). 'Echoing emergence: objectives, rough definitions, and speculations for Echo-Class models' Santa Fe Institute Preprint No: 93-04-023, Santa Fe Institute for the Sciences of Complexity, 1660 Old Pecos Trail, Suite A, Santa Fe, NM 87501, USA.

Holland, J. (1993b). 'The ECHO Model' in Santa Fe Institute 1992 Annual Report, Santa Fe Institute for the Sciences of Complexity, 1660 Old Pecos Trail, Suite A, Santa Fe, NM 87501, USA.

Holland, J. and Langton, C. (1992). 'A computational base for studying complex adaptive systems: Echo and Process Gas', in SFI Proposal for a Research Program in Adaptive Computation, (address as for Holland, 1993a).

Johnson, M. (1987). *The Body in the Mind: The Bodily Basis of Meaning, Imagination, and Reason* (Chicago and London: University of Chicago Press).

Kember, S. (2002). *Humanising Hal. Artificial Life in a Neo-Biological Age* (London and New York, Routledge).

Kirby, V. (1991). 'Corporeal habits: addressing essentialism differently', *Hypatia* 6, pp. 4–24.

Knorr-Cetina, K. (1981). *The Manufacture of Knowledge: An Essay on the Constructivist and Contextual Nature of Science* (Oxford and New York: Pergamon).

Lakoff, G. (1987). *Women, Fire and Dangerous Things: What Categories Reveal About the Mind* (Chicago and London: University of Chicago Press).

Lakoff, G. and Johnson, M. (1980). *Metaphors We Live By* (Chicago: University of Chicago Press).

Lakoff, G. and Johnson, M. (1999). *Philosophy in the Flesh: The Embodied Mind and its Challenge to Western Thought* (New York, Basic Books).

Langton, C. (ed) (1989). *Artificial Life, The Proceedings of an Interdisciplinary Workshop on the Synthesis and Simulation of Living Systems. SFI Studies in the Sciences of Complexity, Vol. VI* (Redwood, Cal.: Addison-Wesley).

Lenat, D. and Guha, R. (1990). *Building Large Knowledge-Based Systems: Representation and Inference in the Cyc Project* (Reading, Mass.: Addison-Wesley).

Lloyd, G. (1984). *The Man of Reason: 'Male' and 'Female' in Western Philosophy* (Minneapolis: University of Minnesota Press).

Nagel, T. (1986). *A View From Nowhere* (Oxford: Oxford University Press).

Rosch, E. (1973). 'Natural categories', *Cognitive Psychology* 4, pp. 328–350.

Rose, H. (1994). *Love, Power and Knowledge: Towards a Feminist Transformation of the Sciences* (Cambridge: Polity Press).

Ruddick, S. (1989). *Maternal Thinking: Towards a Politics of Peace* (Boston, Mass.: Beacon).

Ryle, Gilbert (1963). *The Concept of Mind* (London: Hutchinson).

Searle, J. (1987). 'Minds, brains and programs', in R. Born (ed.) *Artificial Intelligence: The Case Against* (London and Sydney: Croom Helm), (first published 1980), pp. 18–40.

Suchman, L. (1994). 'Supporting articulation work: aspects of a feminist practice of technology production', in A. Adam, J. Emms, E. Green and J. Owen (eds) *IFIP Transactions A-57, Women, Work and Computerization: Breaking Old Boundaries – Building New Forms* (Amsterdam: Elsevier/North-Holland), pp. 7–21.

Wheeler, M. (1996). 'From robots to Rothko: the bringing forth of worlds', in Margaret Boden (ed.) *The Philosophy of Artificial Life* (Oxford: Oxford University Press), pp. 209–236.

Wilson, E. (1975). *Sociobiology: The New Synthesis* (Cambridge, Mass.: Harvard University Press).

Witz, A. (2000). 'Whose body matters? Feminist sociology and the corporeal turn in sociology and feminism', *Body and Society*, 6 (2), pp. 1–24.

Young, I. (1990). 'Throwing like a girl: A phenomenology of feminine body comportment, motility and spatiality' in I. Young (ed.) *Throwing Like a Girl and Other Essays in Feminist Philosophy and Social Theory* (Bloomington and Indianapolis: Indian University Press), pp. 141–159.

4

MERLEAU-PONTY ON THE BODY

Sean Dorrance Kelly

1. Introduction

In the *Phenomenology of Perception*, first published in 1945, Merleau-Ponty describes a patient named Schneider, whose visual pathology stems from a traumatic injury to the brain incurred during trench warfare in the First World War. Schneider's case of morbid motility, according to Merleau-Ponty, 'clearly shows the fundamental relations between the body and space'.[1] The following somewhat lengthy passage occurs near the beginning of Merleau-Ponty's discussion of Schneider:

> In the . . . patient . . . one notices a dissociation of the act of pointing from reactions of taking or grasping: the same subject who is unable to point to order to a part of his body, quickly moves his hand to the point where a mosquito is stinging him. . . . [A]sked to point to some part of his body, his nose for example, [he] can only manage to do so if he is allowed to take hold of it. If the patient is set the task of interrupting the movement before its completion . . . the action becomes impossible. It must therefore be concluded that 'grasping' . . . is different from 'pointing'. From the outset the grasping movement is magically at its completion; it can begin only by anticipating its end, since to disallow taking hold is sufficient to inhibit the action. And it has to be admitted that [even in the case of a normal subject] a point on my body can be present to me as one to be taken hold of without being given in this anticipated grasp as a point to be indicated. But how is this possible? If I know where my nose is when it is a question of holding it, how can I not know where it is when it is a matter of pointing to it?

---

[1] *Phenomenology of Perception*, p. 103.

'It is probably because', Merleau-Ponty concludes, 'knowledge of where something is can be understood in a number of ways'.[2]

The general point of Merleau-Ponty's discussion is that the understanding of space that informs my skillful, unreflective bodily activity – activity such as unreflectively grasping the doorknob in order to go through the door, or skillfully typing at the keyboard – is not the same as, nor can it be explained in terms of, the understanding of space that informs my reflective, cognitive or intellectual acts – acts such as pointing at the doorknob in order to identify it. As Merleau-Ponty says, in skillful, unreflective bodily activity

> my body appears to me as an attitude directed towards a certain existing or possible task. And indeed its spatiality is not . . . *a spatiality of position*, but a *spatiality of situation*.[3]

To give a name to intentional activities that essentially involve our bodily, situational understanding of space and spatial features, Merleau-Ponty coins the phrase 'motor intentionality'. Grasping is the canonical motor-intentional activity.

As recently as 1992, perceptual psychologists were loathe to distinguish between the kind of spatial information available to the visual system for visuo-motor activities such as grasping and the kind available for perceptual judgements about location implicit in acts of pointing. In a forward thinking paper of the day one psychologist writes:

> We often do not differentiate between grasping and pointing when we generalize about how vision is used when generating limb movements. It is possible, that how individuals use vision may vary as a function of whether they are generating pointing or grasping movements, and that some principles of how vision is used during reaching and pointing is (sic) not generalizable to grasping.[4]

This was a maverick view in 1992. Since that time, however, the important work of neuroscientists A. David Milner and Melvyn Goodale has opened the way for acceptance of this basic Merleau-Pontian distinction – the distinction between essentially bodily

[2] *Phenomenology of Perception*, pp. 103–4.
[3] *Phenomenology of Perception*, p. 100.
[4] Carnahan, Heather, 'Eye, head and hand coordination during manual aiming', in Proteau, L. and Elliott, D. (eds.), *Advances in Psychology 85: Vision and Motor Control*, Elsevier Science Publishers B.V., 1992, p. 188.

understandings of space and spatial features, on the one hand, and essentially cognitive or reflective understandings of these on the other. Much of Milner and Goodale's work comes from an analysis of D.F., a patient who suffered carbon monoxide poisoning that resulted in a visual pathology strikingly similar to Schneider's. Milner and Goodale describe her situation as follows:

> D.F.'s ability to recognize or discriminate between even simple geometric forms is grossly impaired. . . . [Her] pattern of visual deficits [however] ... is largely restricted to deficits in form perception. D.F. . . . recovered, within weeks, the ability to reach out and grasp everyday objects with remarkable accuracy. We have discovered recently that she is very good at catching a ball or even a short wooden stick thrown towards her. . . . She negotiates obstacles in her path with ease . . . . These various skills suggest that although D.F. is poor at perceptual report of object qualities such as size and orientation, she is much better at using those same qualities to guide her actions.[5]

In particular, Milner and Goodale report, D.F. is capable of responding differentially to spatial features of an object like its size, shape, and orientation even in cases in which she is incapable of visually identifying those very features. One test of this involved the identification of the orientation of a slot. Quoting again from Milner and Goodale:

> [We] used a vertically mounted disc in which a [rectangular] slot . . . was cut: on different test trials, the slot was randomly set at 0, 45, 90, or 135°. We found that D.F.'s attempts to make a perceptual report of the orientation of the slot showed little relationship to its actual orientation, and this was true whether her reports were made verbally or by manually setting a comparison slot. [Further examination revealed a large variety of other reporting methods for which her performance was equally bad.] Remarkably, however, when she was asked to insert her hand or a hand-held card into the slot from a starting position an arm's length away, she showed no particular difficulty, moving her hand (or the card) towards the slot in the correct orientation and inserting it quite accurately. Video recordings showed that her hand began to rotate in the appropriate direc-

---

[5] *The Visual Brain in Action*, pp. 126–128.

tion as soon as it left the start position. [One is reminded here, by the way, of Merleau-Ponty's claim that 'from the outset the grasping action is magically at its completion'.] In short, although she could not report the orientation of the slot, she could 'post' her hand or a card into it without difficulty.[6]

Milner and Goodale go on to suggest a neurophysiological basis for the dissociation between pointing and grasping. They claim that there are two different streams of visual information flow in the brain, one of which is geared to perceptual judgement, the other of which is geared directly to action. D.F.'s case is one of the principle pieces of evidence that there is not one common understanding of orientation on the basis of which both judgement and action occur, but rather two different ways of understanding spatial qualities like orientation. Indeed, D.F.'s understanding of the orientation of the slot, unlike the more familiar cognitive understanding, is essentially in terms of her bodily capacities and dispositions to act with respect to it. In the terminology of Merleau-Ponty, she has a motor intentional understanding of orientation. In this paper I would like to explore some of the distinctive features of motor intentional activity, and in particular to say something about its logical form.

2. The motor intentional understanding of location

Perhaps a good way to begin to explore the features of motor intentional activity is by comparing them to the features of more cognitive, report oriented modes of understanding an object. The comparison is especially interesting when it comes to the understanding one has of the spatial features of the object like location, size, shape, orientation, and so on. Keeping in line with the discussion so far, I will take grasping an object to be a paradigmatic motor intentional activity, and pointing at an object to be an essentially cognitive, report oriented task. The spatial feature of the object that I will focus on here is its location. Our question, then, will be, What understanding of the location of an object is inherent in the grasping activities directed toward it, and how is this understanding different, if it is, from the understanding of the location of an object on which the pointing act depends? In this section I will argue that, on at least one account

---

[6] *The Visual Brain in Action*, p. 128.

of the understanding of location required for pointing acts, that understanding is neither necessary nor sufficient for the success of grasping activity. If correct, this claim would be for location what Milner and Goodale's analysis suggests about orientation. It would be, in other words, the denial that there is a common understanding of the location of an object in virtue of which both judgements about it and actions toward it occur.

I will think of the pointing act on the model of demonstrative identification. Now, there is a genuine philosophical question about what it is in virtue of which a pointing act picks out or refers to or identifies its object. One widely held view, however, attributable in the first instance to Evans as I understand him, is that the actual location of the object is that in virtue of which the demonstrative pointing act identifies it.[7] By the actual location I mean the location of the object as it is referred to in what is sometimes called an objective cognitive map. The actual location of the object, on this view, is a spatial feature of it that distinguishes the object identified from all other objects in the universe. I will use this general account of pointing, and the spatial features of the object on which its demonstrative identification depends, for the sake of comparison.

In motor intentional activity there is likewise a kind of motor intentional identification of the object – a way of being directed toward it that is in some way dependent upon an understanding of, or at any rate a bodily sensitivity to, its spatial features. This is true at least in the sense that objects of different sizes, shapes, orientations, and locations require different kinds of grasping activities. In the sense of motor intentional identification with which I'll be concerned, successful completion of the relevant motor intentional activity is at least sufficient for motor intentional identification. On this view, then, we can say that D.F. is capable of motor intentionally identifying the orientation of the slot – she has so to speak, a bodily understanding of that orientation – despite the fact that she does not, in a more traditional sense, know what the orientation is. The bodily understanding of a spatial feature of an object is manifest in the subject's capacity to act differentially with respect to that feature.

Whatever this bodily understanding of the object amounts to, however, I believe it is not an understanding of its actual location. Knowledge of the actual location of the object, I claim, is neither

[7] See Evans, *Varieties of Reference.*

necessary nor sufficient for the success of the motor intentional activity directed toward it. I will begin with the denial that knowledge of the actual location of an object is necessary for its motor intentional identification.

For starters, I think there may be an issue of fineness of grain. Suppose that I'm sitting at the breakfast table in the morning and I want to take a sip from my coffee mug, which is at actual location π on the breakfast table. Unreflectively I reach out to grab the mug and, as it happens, I am successful in doing so and in drinking from it. The grasping activity has succeeded in identifying its object motor intentionally. Now the question arises, could the very same activity have succeeded in identifying its object if the mug were in a different actual location? The answer must depend on how we individuate motor intentional activities, and I don't intend to give a general answer to that question here. Surely on some natural criterion we can say that if the actual location were sufficiently different – if the mug were in the middle of Detroit, for example, or maybe even if it were just in the other room – then some different grasping activity would be required. But what if the mug were in an actual location that was different by only a tiny amount – a millimetre, for instance. Suppose that I also succeed in grabbing the mug and drinking from it in this situation. Well, if we make the difference in actual location small enough then on any natural criterion of individuation the activity must be the same. After all, points in actual space are indefinitely small, whereas points in behavioural space must not be. If they were, then motor intentional activity would depend upon factors that are in principle unavailable in any way to the performer of the activity, and this seems to undermine the very notion of a *bodily sensitivity* to the object on the basis of which the activity is performed. So this seems to indicate that an understanding of the very particular actual location of the object is not necessary for the success of motor intentional activity directed toward it.

Perhaps it will be objected, however, that this isn't the kind of knowledge we had in mind when we said that knowledge of the actual location is required for pointing. After all, actual locations of this very particular sort are perceptually indiscriminable in every way, so perhaps knowledge of them is not required for pointing either. One way to proceed at this point, then, is to ask whether the locations with which we identify objects when pointing at them are more finely grained than the locations with which we identify objects when acting with respect to them. I suspect there is a sense in which something like this is true, but I confess that the terrain here is muddy, and that I don't have any good way of drying it up. I will admit, however, that it almost seems to me as though focussing on fineness of grain gets us off on the wrong foot anyway. The real issue is probably not how finely understood the location of the object is, but whether there's anything like a location we understand at all in grasping an object, as opposed to a located object understood as a unitary thing. I'll say a bit more about this in the next section.

For the time being, however, rather than pursue the issue of fineness of grain, I will simply point out that there is another important factor in distinguishing pointing from grasping, one which Evans himself was keen to emphasize. Namely, that the demonstrative pointing act, unlike the grasping activity, cannot succeed unless it is based on knowledge of the object that distinguishes it from every other object in the universe. This is a criterion that is sometimes called 'Russell's Principle', and it is central to both Strawson's and Evans's views on demonstrative identification. But the only way knowledge of the actual location of an object can live up to this demand is if it is knowledge of the object's place in the universe at large, not just knowledge of the object's place with respect to the perceiver. It must be, in Evans's terminology, knowledge of the object's objective location, not just knowledge of its egocentric location. Since only egocentric knowledge is required for grasping, here is a definitive sense in which the understanding of location necessary for pointing is not an understanding that is necessary for the success of motor intentional activity.

I should mention, parenthetically, that this observation leads Evans to develop a view about behavioural or egocentric understandings of space that distinguishes them from objective understandings of space. It's not often noticed, however, that Evans's whole discussion of behavioural space is not only similar to the view about grasping that Merleau-Ponty develops, it is actually motivated by Merleau-Ponty's work. This is clear from the fact that Evans introduces the topic with a long passage from a paper by Charles Taylor in which Taylor is explicitly presenting Merleau-Ponty's view. So it's not surprising that, in a discussion of Merleau-Ponty's account of the body, Evans's views are lurking around.

We have seen, then, that knowledge of the actual location of an object is not necessary for the success of motor intentional activities directed toward it. But knowledge of the actual location is not sufficient for motor intentional identification either. To see this we need only consider parallel situations in which the object is in the same actual location but the success conditions for the motor intentional activity directed toward that object are different. For instance, consider two situations in which my coffee mug is located at actual position π on the breakfast table. In the first of these situations the mug is perched innocently on top of the table, while in the second it is super-glued to the surface. Assuming that in both cases I am grasping the mug in order to drink coffee from it, then it is clear that the conditions for the success of the motor intentional activity in the first case (e.g., that I grasp it normally and drink from it) are different from those in the second case (e.g., that I first pry it off the table top with a crow bar and then grasp it normally and drink from it). Thus, although a normal grasping action is enough properly to identify the mug in the first case (motor intentionally), it is not enough properly to identify it in the second. We could make a similar point by substituting a different object altogether for my coffee mug – a red rubber ball, for instance. Even if it is at the same actual location, a very different kind of grasping activity may be required to grasp the ball successfully than was required to grasp the mug. It seems, then, that motor intentional activities succeed at least partly in virtue of facts about the object toward which they are directed. Because actual locations contain no information about the object that occupies them, knowledge of the actual location alone is insufficient for motor intentional identification.

3. Motor intentionality is an essentially bodily relation to an object

We saw that motor intentional activities succeed at least partly in virtue of facts about the object toward which they are directed. Of course I will change my way of grasping a thing if it's in a substantially different actual location – I'll reach over there instead of over here. But I'll also change my way of grasping it, for instance, if it's a different thing in the same location. What are the differences? I'll form my grip differently, I'll scale my hand opening differently, I may even prepare my entire body differently if the object is perceived to be, for instance, very heavy instead of very light. The upshot is that in identifying an object motor intentionally I typically prepare myself to deal with the entire object, not just with some independently specifiable spatial feature of it, like for instance its actual location. This fact, I believe, is built into the very way we use the terms pointing and grasping, so let me begin by saying something about this.

By contrast first consider the case of pointing. When I point at a table in the corner of the room, I succeed in pointing at the corner of the room whether the table is there or not. If a thief has just ransacked my house I can successfully communicate to the police officer that 'There', (pointing to the corner of the room) 'is where my table used to be'. It is clear when I do this that I am pointing to the same actual location I would have been pointing to had the thief left the table untouched. Since the table is gone, of course, I fail to point at it, but since I am still pointing at the actual location it occupied, it must be the case that this actual location is specifiable independently of the object.

On the other hand, consider grasping. When I grab for my coffee mug in the morning I direct my activity toward it, not simply toward some independent location that it occupies. If I am hallucinating the existence of the mug we do not say that I grasped the location but failed to grasp the object – the grasping activity has failed altogether. The most I can do is grasp at the (actual) location, but if there's no object there, it won't be a genuine grasping act. Genuine grasping, it seems, is directed not just toward a location, but toward a located object.

The perceived existence of the object is so important to the grasping act that without it the action is measurably distinct. This is clear from another interesting empirical result, this one reported by Goodale, Jakobson, and Keillor.[8] These authors have shown that there are measurable qualitative differences between natural grasping movements directed toward an actual object and 'pantomimed' movements directed toward a remembered object. When an actual object is present to be grasped, the subjects typically scale their hand opening for object size and form their grip to correspond to the shape of the object. In pantomimed actions, on the other hand, when there is no object present, although the subjects continue to scale their hand opening, their grip formation differs significantly from that seen in normal target directed

    [8] Goodale, Jakobson, Keillor, 'Differences in the visual control of pantomimed and natural grasping movements.', *Neuropsychologia*, Oct., 1994, v. 32 (n. 10), pp. 1159–1178.

actions. It seems that the actual perceived presence of a thing, and not just some independent representation of it (like a memory), is necessary for the motor intentional activity directed toward it. This is why Merleau-Ponty insists that motor intentional activity is directed toward the object itself in all its particularity. As he says,

> In the action of the hand which is raised towards an object is contained a reference to the object, not as an object represented, but as that *highly specific thing* towards which we project ourselves, near which we are, in anticipation, and which we haunt.[9]

This is not merely the kind of direct realism that is sometimes found in the philosophical literature nowadays. That's because it's not just the rejection of representational intermediaries; it is also an embrace of the positive notion of a whole bodily understanding of the object.

It is important to emphasize again, therefore, that the understanding of the entire object that I have when I am grasping it is not an understanding I can have independent of my bodily activity with respect to it. My bodily activity with respect to the object just is my way of understanding it. We saw this already in the case of D.F. – the understanding of the orientation of the slot that she has in posting a card through it is not an understanding she can have independent of the posting activity. In particular hers is not the kind of understanding of orientation that she can report in any way other than by actually posting the card through the oriented slot. But this kind of bodily understanding of the world is familiar to normal subjects as well. Merleau-Ponty gives the example of a typist's bodily understanding of the keyboard:

> To know how to type is not, then, to know the place of each letter among the keys, nor even to have acquired a conditioned reflex for each one, which is set in motion by the letter as it comes before our eye. If [bodily skill] is neither a form of knowledge nor an involuntary action, what then is it? It is knowledge in the hands, which is forthcoming only when bodily effort is made, and cannot be formulated in detachment from that effort.[10]

That there is a peculiarly bodily type of understanding of

---

[9] Merleau-Ponty, *Phenomenology of Perception*, p. 138, italics in the original.
[10] *Phenomenology of Perception*, p. 144.

objects is the central point of Merleau-Ponty's category of motor
intentionality: motor intentional activity is a way of being directed
toward objects that essentially involves a motor or behavioural
component. As Merleau-Ponty says in introducing the phrase:

> . . . we are brought to the recognition of something between
> [reflex] movement as a third person process and thought as a
> representation of movement – something which is an anticipa-
> tion of, or arrival at, the objective and is ensured by the body
> itself as a motor power, a 'motor project' (*Bewegungsentwurf*), a
> 'motor intentionality' . . .[11]

In motor intentional activity, in other words, there is not an
independent way we have of understanding the object on the
basis of which we act differentially with respect to it. Rather our
bodily activity is itself a kind of understanding of the object. This
is surely an odd kind of understanding of the world, and I don't
claim to have clarified it much beyond insisting that it is essentially bodily. But in the next, and final, section I will try to show
that if we take this idea seriously, then the logical form of motor
intentional activity is very different from that of more traditional
cognitive or reflective intentional states. Although this still won't
tell us what motor intentional identification is, it will give a pretty
good idea of how strange a thing it must be.

4. The logical form of motor intentional activity

The claim I'm interested in is this: that the logical form of motor
intentional activity is different from the logical form of cognitive
or reflective intentional states, states such as believing that John is
in the bedroom, hoping that the sun will shine, or intending to
buy the flowers. In particular, the difference is that it is impossible to distinguish the content of motor intentional activity from
the attitude directed toward that content. The content/attitude
distinction is perhaps the most basic logical distinction one can
make in the characterization of cognitive or reflective intentional
states. The claim that motor intentional activity fails to admit such
a distinction, therefore, if correct, will serve to distinguish motor
intentionality from reflective intentionality in a relatively formal
and complete way.

One standard way to characterize a belief state is in terms of a

---

[11] *ibid.*, p. 110.

proposition consisting of concepts possessed by the subject enjoying the belief. If Sally believes that the slot is oriented at 45°, for instance, then we may say that Sally possesses the concepts [slot] and [oriented at 45°]. At a minimum this means that she is capable of entertaining at least some other thoughts involving these concepts – thoughts about slots that are not oriented at 45°, for instance, and thoughts about things other than slots that are so oriented. The proposition consisting of the concepts [slot] and [oriented at 45°] is a representation of the way the world is toward which Sally has the attitude of belief.

But what is the content – the representation of the way the world is – that is at play in D.F.'s motor intentional activity? It is clear that it is not a representation that contains the concept [oriented at 45°]. In the first place, it is unlikely that D.F. even possesses such a concept. She is systematically incapable of reporting that things are oriented at 45° when they are, and this seems at least a pretty good first-order guide to whether she possesses the concept or not. It is possible, I suppose, that she possesses the concept by deference – the way some of us may possess the concept [arthritis] by deferring to experts in our community, despite the fact that we systematically misapply the term ourselves. But even if she does possess the concept by deference, she is certainly not making use of somebody else's knowledge when she posts the card through the oriented slot. So it is clear that she is not in any way using the concept [oriented at 45°] in performing the motor intentional activity of posting the card through the slot that is, as a matter of fact, oriented at 45°. If there is a representational content that characterizes her understanding of the orientation of the slot, then, it must not be one containing the concept [oriented at 45°].

The problem is that there seems to be no concept that D.F. possesses in virtue of which she is capable of performing the posting activity. It's not merely that she can't count to 45, for instance, and for that reason fails to possess the concept [oriented at 45°], but she possesses some other extensionally equivalent concept. No, she also can't draw the slope of the slot on a piece of paper or even rotate her hand into the correct orientation without at the same time moving it toward the slot. She seems, in other words, not to be able to represent the orientation of the slot at all except by means of posting the card through it. This is another way of putting the claim that motor intentional activities constitute essentially bodily understandings of their objects.

But still, why can't we think of this activity itself as a way of under-standing the orientation of the slot toward which she can have the attitude of belief? Why can't she say, in other words, 'I believe the slot is oriented *this* way [said while posting the card through the slot]'? Well, she can say this, I think, and I understand from Goodale that she's learned to make use of this technique. Indeed, he says it's made experiments very tricky recently. The problem is, if you ask her to report the orientation of the slot, she'll begin to move her hand toward the slot as if she were going to push it through, and then at the last moment she'll stop, saying '*This* is the orientation it's in' [rigidly holding her hand in its final position]. Now it's true, in this instance, that she has a representation of orientation that she can report. She has a representational content, in other words, toward which she can have the attitude of belief. But the question is whether this is the representation of the orien-tation of the slot that constituted the understanding she had of it when she was posting the card through the slot. I suspect it's not.

The difference, I think, is that when she stops the posting action, the thought she has then seems to be about whatever orientation her hand happens to be in. I strongly suspect, for instance, that if you changed the orientation of the slot after she'd stopped moving her hand, and didn't let her begin the post-ing activity again, she would continue to say that the orientation of the slot is whatever orientation her hand ended up in. What is revealed in the posting activity, however, is the actual orientation of the slot – it's that orientation itself that the activity is sensitive to. So even if she can have an attitude toward the activity that manifests an understanding of the orientation, this is not the same as having an attitude toward the understanding of the orien-tation that the activity manifests.

The situation is a bit like the one that Frege describes with respect to the concept horse. For Frege, any attempt to refer to the concept horse *as a concept* will necessarily fail, since referring to it at all turns it into an object. So too, it seems, any attempt to characterize as an independently specifiable representation the understanding of orientation that D.F. manifests in her posting activity will necessarily turn it into a different kind of under-standing than the kind it was at the time of the performance. The understanding of orientation that the activity manifests, in other words, seems not to be the kind of thing toward which we can have an attitude at all.

Supposing this is true for D.F., we might wonder whether it is

true for ourselves as well. I suspect it is. Consider the understanding of the doorknob that you have when you unreflectively
reach out to open the door. Is this understanding itself the kind
of understanding toward which you can have an attitude? Or is
it rather the case that in order to reflect upon the understanding manifest in the activity at all we necessarily change it into
something different from what it was at the time the activity was
being performed? It is more difficult to know in our case, since
unlike D.F. we do possess concepts like orientation, size, shape,
location, and so on, and it's tempting to re-construct the understanding manifest in our activity in terms of these. But is it in
virtue of this kind of conceptual understanding of the object
that we perform our unreflective, skillful activities? If Milner
and Goodale are right in hypothesizing that there is an independent stream of visual information that is directly tied to
action, then perhaps this kind of motor intentional understanding even for normal subjects is a kind that we cannot
reflectively access as such. We may be able to reflect on the
activity itself of course – I sometimes seem to be able to remember, for instance, reaching out to grasp the doorknob, even if I
wasn't aware of doing it when I actually performed the activity.
But again, this seems to be reflecting on the activity, not on the
understanding of the doorknob that's manifest in it. So there
seems to be good evidence for thinking that motor intentional
activity is like this even for normal subjects, that it essentially
discloses the world to us, in other words, but cannot be
captured in the process of doing so. This coheres with
Schneider's report of his own experience, which is a kind of
pure motor intentionality, for he says,

> I experience the movements as being a result of the situation,
> of the sequence of events themselves; myself and my move-
> ments are, so to speak, merely a link in the whole process and
> I am scarcely aware of any voluntary initiative. . . . It all happens
> independently of me.[12]

Because motor-intentional activity is called forth by the situation in this way, and is therefore to some degree independent of
the autonomous will of the subject, it does not have at its heart
the kind of autonomous representational content that a subject
could have an attitude toward. I suspect that this is the point that

---

[12] *Phenomenology of Perception*, p. 105.

Merleau-Ponty was trying to make in this final passage with which I'll end. Merleau-Ponty writes:

> [I]f I can, with my left hand, feel my right hand as it touches an object, the right hand as an object is not the right hand as it touches: the first is a system of bones, muscles and flesh brought down at a point of space, the second shoots through space like a rocket to reveal the external object in its place. In so far as it sees or touches the world, my body can therefore be neither seen nor touched. What prevents its ever being an object [like any other], ever being 'completely constituted', is that it is that by which there are objects [for us]. [But] it is neither tangible nor visible in so far as it is that which sees and touches. . . . [Therefore] the body [must] no longer [be] conceived [strictly] as an object of the world, but as our means of communication with it, to the world not longer conceived as a collection of determinate objects, but as the horizon latent in all our experience and itself ever-present and anterior to every determining thought.[13]

References

Carnahan, Heather. (1992). 'Eye, head and hand coordination during manual aiming', in Proteau, L. and Elliott, D. (eds.), *Advances in Psychology 85: Vision and Motor Control* (Elsevier Science Publishers B.V).

Evans, Gareth. (1982). *Varieties of Reference* (Oxford: Oxford University Press).

Goodale, Jakobson, Keillor. (1994). 'Differences in the visual control of pantomimed and natural grasping movements.', *Neuropsychologia*, 32, 1159–1178.

Merleau-Ponty, Maurice (1962). *Phenomenology of Perception*, C. Smith, trans. (London: Routledge & Kegan Paul).

Milner, A. David and Goodale, Melvyn A. (1995). *The Visual Brain in Action*, Oxford: Oxford University Press.

---

[13] *Phenomenology of Perception*, p. 92.

5

SAMUEL TODES'S ACCOUNT OF NON-CONCEPTUAL PERCEPTUAL KNOWLEDGE AND ITS RELATION TO THOUGHT

Hubert L. Dreyfus

I. Introduction

In *Body and World*,[1] Samuel Todes starts with Merleau-Ponty's general description of the motor intentionality of the lived body, and goes on to develop a detailed description of the structure of the active body and of the role that that structure plays in producing the spatio-temporal field of experience. He then examines how the spatio-temporal field makes possible 'objective knowledge' of the objects that show up in it. Todes's goal is to show that perception involves non-conceptual, but, nonetheless, objective forms of judgment. Thus, one can think of *Body and World*, as fleshing out Merleau-Ponty's project while relating it to the current scene.

Todes's work draws on two connected intellectual movements brought to the United States in the 40s by German refugees: Gestalt Psychology and Phenomenology. The connection between them was first pointed out in the 20s by Aron Gurwitsch.[2] Gurwitsch worked closely with Husserl documenting this similarity until the Nazis came to power in 1933. He then spent seven years in Paris lecturing on the confluence of Gestalt Psychology and Transcendental Phenomenology, where his lectures were attended by Maurice Merleau-Ponty.[3] Merleau-Ponty subsequently transposed Gurwitsch's Husserlian phenomenology of perception into his own existential account of the role of the lived body in experience.[4]

---

[1] Todes, Samuel, *Body and World* (MIT Press, 2001). (Page references are included in brackets after quotations.)

[2] Gurwitsch's dissertation subject was 'Studies in the Relation between Gestalt Psychology and Phenomenology'. See also his, *The Field of Consciousness* (Duquesne University Press, 1964).

[3] For details on Gurwitsch's relationship with Merleau-Ponty see Lester E. Embree's 'Biographical Sketch' in *Life-World and Consciousness: Essays for Aron Gurwitsch* (Northwestern University Press, 1972).

[4] Merleau-Ponty, Maurice, *Phénoménologie de la perception* (Paris: Éditions Gallimard, 1945). Translation: *Phenomenology of Perception*. C. Smith, trans. (London: Routledge & Kegan Paul, 1962).

Todes carries forward existential phenomenology by elaborating the Gestalt description of the field of consciousness proposed by Gurwitsch, while giving an account of the role of the lived body in perception and action that goes beyond the work of Merleau-Ponty. Thus, Todes's book can be seen as the latest development in the philosophical movement that leads from Köhler and Husserl, to Gurwitsch, and then to Merleau-Ponty.

II. Are there two kinds of knowledge?

The philosophical tradition, has generally assumed, or, in the case of Kant, argued persuasively, that there is only one kind of intelligibility, the unified understanding we have of things when we make judgements that objectify our experience by bringing it under concepts. But there have always been others – painters, writers, historians, linguists, philosophers in the romantic tradition, Wittgensteinians, and existential phenomenologists – who have felt that there is another kind of intelligibility that gets us in touch with reality besides the conceptual kind elaborated by Kant.

Todes enters this debate by opposing the intelligibility of conception and perception. He sums up his project as follows:

> Kant [does justice] neither to the claims of conceptual imagination nor to the claims of perception. Our solution is to show that there are two levels of objective experience: the ground floor of perceptually objective experience; and the upper storey of imaginatively objective experience . . . We attempt to show *that* the imaginative objectivity of theoretical knowledge presupposes a pre-imaginative, perceptual form of objectivity, by showing just *how* this is so (p. 100).

Todes's proposed approach is timely. Donald Davidson holds that there is nothing more philosophers can say about perception than that it causes us to have beliefs and other attitudes that are directed towards the world. John McDowell, in *Mind and World*, answers that we can say at least this much more, viz. that, for perception to enter into the space of reasons, it must have conceptual content 'all the way out'. As he puts it:

> To avoid making it unintelligible how the deliverances of sensibility can stand in grounding relations to paradigmatic exercises of the understanding such as judgments and beliefs, . . . we must insist that the understanding is already inextricably

implicated in the deliverances of sensibility themselves. Experiences are impressions made by the world on our senses, products of receptivity; but those impressions themselves already have conceptual content.[5]

Neither Davidson nor McDowell tries to describe perceptual objects as they are perceived and explain how they become the objects of thought. By calling attention to the structure of non-conceptual, practical perception and showing how its judgments can be transformed into the judgments of detached thought, Todes is able to provide a framework in which to explain how the content of perception, while not itself conceptual, can provide the basis for conception. Thus, Todes's *Body and World* can be read as a significant response to McDowell's *Mind and World*.

III. Practical perception as a distinct kind of knowledge

Todes's account of the nature of non-conceptual content builds on the work of Merleau-Ponty. Merleau-Ponty claims that, in perceiving things, I usually sense that they could be more clearly perceived and my body is drawn to get a firmer grip on them.

> My body is geared to the world when my perception offers me a spectacle as varied and as clearly articulated as possible, and when my motor intentions, as they unfold, receive from the world the responses they anticipate. This maximum distinctness in perception and action defines a perceptual ground, a basis of my life, a general milieu for the coexistence of my body and the world.[6]

In Todes's terms, we are always trying to cope more effectively, and our perception of the things around us is a response to our dissatisfaction with our lostness in the world. We find ourselves by moving so as to organize a stable spatio-temporal field in which we use our skills to make determin*ate* the determin*able* objects that appear in that field. The skills we acquire then feed back into the perceptual world, which becomes more and more determinate as we learn to make more refined discriminations and thus have more reliable anticipations. Merleau-Ponty calls this feedback phenomenon the *intentional arc.*

---

[5] McDowell, John, *Mind and World* (Harvard University Press, 1994, p. 46).
[6] Merleau-Ponty, Maurice, *Phenomenology of Perception*, pp. 49–50.

But, one might well object, the objects of our perception do not look indeterminate. To explain how perception hides its essential indeterminacy, Todes introduces a phenomenological account of need. A *need*, whether it be for getting a maximal grip or a more specific need, is at first experienced as an indeterminate deprivation; not a simple absence. This distinction, according to Todes, is the difference between *perceptual negation* as a positive lack that calls for a response, and *logical negation* as the absence of something specific that might have been present.

In moving to meet a need, the perceiver makes both the need and the object that meets that need sufficiently determinate so that the need can be satisfied. The perceiver then understands the object as that determinate object that was needed all along. As Todes puts it:

> The retroactive determination of needs by their being met covers up the fact that they first become determinate by being met. The meeting of a need first fixes it; but it is fixed retroactively as having been that determinate need all along (p. 178).

Thus, although perception is temporal, moving from lack to satisfaction and from indeterminacy to relative determination, after the act is completed, the dissatisfaction and the object that satisfied it are experienced as having all along been completely determinate.[7]

A similar tendency to read back into everyday coping the transformation that such coping bring about, takes place in our experience of acting. When Todes describes our absorbed, skilful coping, he is clear that in acting we are not trying to achieve a goal that can be spelled out in advance in propositional form. Absorbed coping does not require that the agent's movements be governed by a representation of the action's success conditions, as John Searle, for example, claims.[8] Todes agrees with Merleau-Ponty who maintains that, in absorbed coping, the agent's body is led to move so as to reduce a sense of deviation from a satisfactory gestalt without the agent being able to represent what that satisfactory gestalt will be like in advance of achieving it.

---

[7] The indeterminacy of perceptual objects and their dependence on various situational and bodily capacities is argued for in detail in Sean D Kelly, 'The non-conceptual content of perceptual experience: situation dependence and fineness of grain', *Philosophy and Phenomenological Research* (with response by Christopher Peacocke), vol. LXII, no. 3 (May, 2001).

[8] Searle, John R. *Intentionality* (Cambridge: Cambridge University Press, 1983), p. 90.

Merleau-Ponty calls the embodied coping that is directed toward objects under aspects but has no propositional success conditions, '*motor intentionality*'. Todes calls this non-conceptual, on-going coping, *poise*.[9] He notes that, 'the primary form of directed action is an intention of the *body*. . . . This intention of the active body is *poise* in dealing with the things and persons around us' (p. 65). Todes, however, goes further than Merleau-Ponty. He not only distinguishes the *expected success conditions* of wilful trying from the on-going *satisfaction of the anticipations* of poised perception; he adds that the continuing activity of on-going coping gives us *perceptual knowledge* of the things with which we are coping.

> My response to an anticipated object reveals to me directly, merely by virtue of its existence, not merely the self-produced movements of my own body by which I make that response, but also, and equally immediately, that thing in respect to which I have been able to make the response. This is not true if I construe the primary form of directed action on the model of an act of will, . . . so that I must await the effect of actions to see whether they coincide with my previously definite intentions . . . . Poise does not, when successful, 'coincide' or 'agree' with its later 'effects', as does will with its achievements. . . . The success of poise is not in its *execution*, but in its very *existence*, by which the body is, to begin with, knowingly in touch with the objects around it. As soon as I am poised in my circumstances, I know . . . something about those objects to which I am doing something with my body (pp. 65–66).

For example, I can't be skilfully coping, say dribbling a basketball, unless I am responding to the position and movement of the actual object. Successful on-going coping is, thus, itself a kind of knowledge.[10]

Trying to achieve *conditions of satisfaction* only occurs when the flow of on-going coping is somehow disturbed.

> When I act in an effective, poised way, it is not merely that what I was trying to do is in *agreement* with what I (distinguishably)

---

[9] 'Poise', which usually describes a static stance, is a rather misleading term for the way a skilled perceiver moves successfully to lower the tension produced in him by the indeterminacy or disequilibrium in his perceptual field. The reader must always keep in mind that, for Todes, poise is a characteristic of skilful *activity*.

[10] Merleau-Ponty sees this phenomenon, but doesn't draw out the epistemological consequences.

did. Rather, . . . there were not two things to compare, but only
the *perfect fit* of me-in-my circumstances. . . . It is only in failure
of response, and loss of poise, that a distinction appears
between what I was trying to do and what I did (p. 70).

The retroactive transformation that occurs in the conversion of
absorbed coping into wilful trying will be a helpful guide in understanding what happens in perception when the non-conceptual is
converted into the conceptual. When my non-conceptual coping
skill fails, and I have to make an effort to bring about what my skill
should have effortlessly accomplished, it seems that, since I am
trying to achieve the same end my skill was directed towards, I must
have been trying to achieve that end all along. But, on careful
reflection, it should be clear that trying does not simply make
explicit *a wilful effort* to achieve a *goal* – both of which were already
there but unnoticed. If a doorknob sticks and I have to make an
effort to turn it, that does not show that I had been *trying* to turn it
all along, i.e. that my movements have been caused by my entertaining those success conditions, any more than it shows that I
believed that turning the doorknob would enable me to open the
door or that I *expected* the door to open, even though I did, indeed,
anticipate its opening in the way my body was set to walk though it.
The transformation from non-conceptual, absorbed anticipations
to attentive goal-directed action introduces a new element, the
conceptual representation of my goal.[11]

A further, more fundamental, dependence of the conceptual
on the non-conceptual arises from the way both absorbed
coping and attentive trying are dependent on the spatio-temporal field organized by the body. That field is produced by the
way the body's specific structure constrains and enables its
coping skills.

To understand Todes's contribution here one must first
understand that the lived body is not the objective body,
compose of muscles, sense organs, a brain, etc., studied by
science. But it is not the subjective body either. It is important to be clear from the outset that Todes, like Merleau-Ponty,
is not interested in how we feel our body when we turn our
attention to it as passive contemplators in meditation, or even
when we introspect the specific kinaesthetic sensations that
accompany specific bodily movements. Each of these modes of

---

[11] For details, see Hubert L. Dreyfus, 'A Merleau-Pontian Critique of Husserl's and
Searle's Representationalist Accounts of Action', *Proceedings of the Aristotelian Society* (2000).

reflection blocks insight into our unreflective experience of our *active* body.[12]

According to Merleau-Ponty and Todes, we do, indeed, experience our active body, but when things are going well, we do not do so by monitoring on bodily sensations. The kinaesthetic sensations we can become aware of on reflection, tell us, in a context free way, the location, motion, etc. of each of our body's parts. But, for Merleau-Ponty and Todes, we normally experience our active body as does an athlete in flow; that is, we sense it transparently responding as a whole to the whole situation. Todes points out that

> we have . . . three phenomenological ordered levels of awareness of our active body. We sense the *skilfulness* of our body-activity in respect to circumstantial objects, as founded in the *coordination* of the activity of our various body-members in respect to one another, and this in turn as founded in the felt *unity* of our active body (p. 206).

It might seem that, in this quotation, Todes is claiming precisely that we do experience the location and movement of our separate body parts in order to coordinate them, but this would be like claiming that when we experience perceptual objects we experience sensations of separate qualities such as colour, shape, texture, etc. and then combine them in a judgement – a view that both Merleau-Ponty and Todes, following the Gestaltists, reject. Rather, Todes is saying that our sense of our active body's unity is prior to, and organizes, our sense of the coordination of our body's members.

To make his case that the structure of the active body plays a crucial role in structuring the spatio-temporal field, Todes has to go beyond Merleau-Ponty's account of the lived body as a unified capacity for action that responds to the world's solicitations. He does this by describing in detail just how the specific structure of our active body produces our unified experience of space and time.

Todes points out that, as the body moves forward more effectively than backwards, it opens a *horizontal field* that organizes experience into what can be coped with directly, what can be

---

[12] For an egregious example of the former type of misunderstanding of Merleau-Ponty see Varela, F. J., Thompson, E. & Rosch, E. (1991) *The embodied mind: Cognitive science and human experience* (MIT Press). For a misunderstanding of the latter type, see Maxine Sheets-Johnstone, *The Roots of Thinking* (Temple University Press, 1990).

reached with effort, and what is over the perceptual horizon. Furthermore, the front/back asymmetry of the active body, viz. that it can cope well only with what is in front of it, makes the horizontal field temporal. In everyday coping, what has yet to be faced is experienced as in the future, what is being faced and dealt with makes up the pragmatic present, and what already has been faced and is behind us is experienced as both spatially and temporally passed. Todes concludes:

> Thus through movement we do not merely notice but produce the spatio-temporal field around us, our circumstantial field, the field in which things appear to us (p. 49).[13]

Next Todes argues that, since perceptual objects can be experienced only in a spatio-temporal field, they can never be given as fully determinate. Rather, a perceptual object has a front and a back and an inside and an outside, so that any particular experience of such an object 'perceptually implies'[14] hidden aspects soliciting further exploration and determination. For example, what I take to be a house seen from the front *looks* like a *house* not a *façade*. It is not as if I see what looks like a house front and I then *infer* that it has a back and inside. In confronting what I take to be a house, my body is solicited to go around it, while, if I take it I am seeing a façade, I embody no such readiness. Thus, while a house looks thick and as if it conceals rooms to be discovered upon further exploration, a façade, looks thin, and seems to hide only empty terrain. One, thus, has non-conceptual perceptual 'beliefs' about perceptual objects, e.g. one of my 'beliefs', in seeing a *house*, is my being set to walk through the front door. The intentional content of such a perceptual belief is in the motor intentionality of my bodily set, that is, in the way I am prepared to act, and do act if nothing intervenes.

This description casts an interesting light on an ongoing debate between Barry Stroud and John McDowell.[15] Stroud, believes with Davidson that beliefs can only be justified by other

---

[13] But, although the structure of the spatio-temporal field depends on the structure of the lived body, Todes is no idealist. In Introduction II to Todes's *Body and World* Piotr Hoffman shows how the fundamental phenomenon of balance, which is so close to us that no previous phenomenologist has described it, enables Todes to argue that the vertical field is given as independent of our action, and so to avoid the antirealism that threatens the philosophies of both Heidegger and Merleau-Ponty.

[14] Gurwitsch coined this expression. Todes uses the term on p. 196.

[15] The discussion took place in a seminar given by McDowell in Berkeley, March 9, 2001.

beliefs, and that therefore appeals to the given can never do any justificatory work. So, on Stroud's view, seeing a green ball involves believing and judging that I am being presented with a green ball. McDowell, anxious to avoid *pure spontaneity* which would seem to leave our beliefs and judgements unconnected with the world and so hanging in the void, counters with the Muller-Lyer illusion, and claims that, in seeing the illusion as an illusion, I am purely *receptive.* I do not judge that one line is longer than the other. Stroud, however, thinks I must be doing more than just gaping at the line; I must be judging something, perhaps that one line *looks* longer. But that, of course, would be a judgement about my experience, not about what's in the world. The most McDowell will admit is that I am being tempted to judge that one line is longer, but he holds that, since I neither believe one line is longer nor that it is not, I am not judging at all. To the phenomenologist, it looks like holding that the only alternatives for describing perception are pure receptivity or pure spontaneity, leads to an antinomy in which the implausibility of each view seems to lend support to its denial.

If we accept the embodied account of perception offered by Merleau-Ponty and Todes, however, we have a third option. Unless I am in a special philosophical attitude of pure contemplation, when I perceive something, my body responds to whatever is presented by being set to act appropriately. We can thus see that our active body's response to what is presented is, neither pure sensory receptivity nor pure spontaneous mental activity, but a *readiness to respond.* Of course, this does not solve the problem both Stroud and McDowell are trying to deal with, viz. how perception can justify beliefs, but Todes's phenomenology does suggest that getting a more accurate account of perception would be a step towards getting an answer.

According to Todes, we can begin to answer the question of the relation of perception to reasons by noting that we make *perceptual inferences* and form *perceptual judgments.* To take a Merleau-Pontian example, on the basis of past experience with similar boxes, one might mistakenly see a belted box as heavy, with the 'perceptual implication' that lifting it would require an effort, that is I would normally be set to use more force than necessary to pick it up. My readiness to use such force would be a mistaken 'perceptual judgment.'

Philosophers generally agree with Aristotle and Kant that, in making a judgment, we subsume a particular under a general concept. In a *perceptual* judgment, however, although our set to lift the object is similar to our set for lifting other heavy objects, we bring to bear a specific body-set, in the example a set to lift this particular heavy object in this particular situation. As Sean Kelly puts this important point, one cannot *specify* the perceiver's practical knowledge of an object independent of the perceiver's actual disposition to cope with it.[16]

IV. Perceptual content is non-conceptual

We are now ready to see that motor intentionality has non-conceptual content. McDowell proposes as a test for *conceptual* content that its objects must be reidentifiable.[17] He says:

> We can ensure that what we have in view is genuinely recognizable as a conceptual capacity if we insist that the very same capacity to embrace a colour in mind can in principle persist beyond the duration of the experience itself.

McDowell doesn't speak of 're-identification'. However, Sean Kelly argues that McDowell's 'recognitional capacity' gives rise to a reidentification criterion.[18] The reidentification criterion states that, for a subject to possess a concept of an object or property 'x', the subject must be able consistently to re-identify a given object or property as falling under that concept if it does.

To determine whether the content of *perceptual* attitudes is an alternative and irreducible kind of content, we must, therefore, ask: Does the content of motor intentionality pass the reidentification test? It is crucial, in answering this question, to realize that, as Todes points out, when objects are made determinate by skilful coping, it is our whole, unified body that gets a grip on the whole unified object in a specific unified context:

> In the last analysis, . . . we can have an object in perception only by our whole perceptual field and all its contents being sensed as centred in the felt unity of our active body (p. 206).

So Todes argues that, just as practical perception involves its own sort of implications, beliefs, judgements and knowledge, it

---

[16] I owe this way of putting the point to Sean D Kelly. See, 'What do we see (when we do)?' in *Philosophical Topics*, vol. 27, no. 2, (Fall/Winter 1999).

[17] McDowell, John, *Mind and World*, p. 57.

[18] See Kelly's 'Demonstrative concepts and experience', *Philosophical Review*, Vol. 110, No. 3 (July 2001).

has its own nonconceptual form of reidentification. In thought, I can reidentify an object as the same object in a wide variety of possible contexts. So, for example, I recognize a chair by subsuming it under the general concept chair and can then reidentify it in any context as long as I retain that concept. In practical perception, on the contrary, my 'reidentification' does not depend on the intellectual act of *recognizing* that this is the same object I have encountered in other situations; it consists simply in my coping with the object in a way that is *in fact* similar to the way I have coped with it on other occasions.[19]

I may, for example, have a body-set to deal with a particular chair in my office, and, although, that particular body-set is in fact similar to my set for dealing with other chairs, and with this chair on other occasions, I needn't experience this chair *as* similar to other chairs or *as* identical with the one I sat on yesterday. I can be simply disposed to sit in it, in this situation, in my usual stiff or relaxed or seductive way. I perceptually *identify* the chair I'm about to sit on as my office chair simply by being set to sit in it in the way I usually sit in my office chair. I don't *reidentify* it as a chair that I have encountered in other possible contexts. Indeed, while I can *conceptually reidentify* the chair in my office as an instance of a type of chair and as having certain characteristics that would enable me to recognize it even on the street, my *perceptual identification* of the chair in my office is so concrete, contextual, and tied to my current disposition to cope with it that it does not follow that I could perceptually reidentify it in other possible contexts.

Just as the body set involved in the practical perception of an object is too responsive to the specific *external* context to assure reidentification in other contexts, the body set for coping with the whole object makes it impossible to isolate the various characteristics of the object from their *internal* context as characteristics of that specific object. The characteristics of a perceptual object are, therefore, not experienced as *isolable features* that could

---

[19] In this connection it's interesting to note that, although persons with Anteriograde Amnesia (such as in the film *Memento*) cannot learn anything explicitly, they are able to acquire skills, both cognitive and motor, at the same rate as normal subjects. For example, one might bring one of the patients into the lab, explain Rubik's cube to them, and have them solve it. Maybe the first day, it takes one hour. The second day, they might solve it in a 1/2 hour, but not remember having seen the puzzle before. The learning curve is the same as normals, but they do not have any explicit recognition of the task and, of course, do not reidentify the cube conceptually, although they must reidentify it in a practical perceptual way.

be features of other possible objects, but, rather, as the *aspects* of that particular object. Todes points out that we always perceive *aspects of an object.* Merleau-Ponty, makes the same point, when he says:

> It is impossible to understand perception as the imputation of a certain significance to certain sensible signs, since the most immediate sensible texture of these signs cannot be described without referring to the object they signify.[20]

In this connection Merleau-Ponty speaks of seeing the woolly-blueness of a carpet.[21] That is, given the perceiver's current coping capacities (which are based on skills formed in prior experiences with this carpet), the carpet looks to be a blue rich with perceptual implications, as one's body is set to feel the carpet's particular flexibility, weight, warmth, fuzziness, etc. On the basis of other past experiences and their correlated body-set, a block of ice would presumably look a slick-hard-cold-blue. In general, the experience of any characteristic of an object of practical perception is tied to the perceiver's holistic body-set. As Merleau-Ponty notes:

> Cézanne said that one could see the velvetiness, the hardness, the softness, and even the odour of objects. My perception is therefore not a sum of visual, tactile, and audible givens: I perceive in a total way with my whole being; I grasp a unique structure of the thing, a unique way of being, which speaks to all my senses at once.[22]

Thus, the aspects of the objects of practical perception, such as the woolly-warm-flexible-blueness of this carpet, are so contextually determined that they cannot be seen as the features of other possible objects, and so could not be reidentified in a different object; yet the perceiver's anticipations are determinate enough to have conditions of satisfaction. That is, the perceiver anticipates the experience of this warm-flexible-blue carpet. It follows that the intentional content by means of which the aspects of perceptual objects are perceived must be non-conceptual.

---

[20] Merleau-Ponty, Maurice, 'The Film and the New Psychology', in *Sense and Non-sense,* trans. Hubert L. Dreyfus and Patricia Allen Dreyfus (Chicago, Northwestern University Press, 1964), p. 51.

[21] Merleau-Ponty develops this Gestalt account of the 'synaesthesia' of perception in *Phenomenology of Perception,* see especially pp. 229 and 313.

[22] Maurice Merleau-Ponty, 'The Film and the New Psychology', p. 50.

But, that leaves us with the troubling question: If perception is, indeed, holistic and non-conceptual all the way in, how are we able to entertain propositional beliefs about isolable perceptual objects and their isolable properties and, more generally, how is thought able to make judgments on the basis of perceptual experience?

The objects of thought must be context-free objects and the context-free properties of such objects, but it is important to see that, just as in absorbed coping there is neither an act of trying nor a representation of a goal, so, in practical perception, I do not encounter context-independent objects nor reidentifiable *properties* or *features* of the object I am perceiving. But if the context-free and thus reidentifiable objects and properties that thought takes up are neither perceptual objects nor the aspects of perceptual objects, how do the objects of practical perception become the objects of abstract thought?

V. How perception is related to thought

According to Todes, the transformation of *contextually determined perceptual* objects with *integrated aspects* into *decontextualized conceptual* objects with *isolable features* takes place in two stages. To begin with, the spectatorial attitude, by deactivating one's bodily set to cope, transforms the integrated *aspects* of the perceptual object into a set of isolable *qualities*. To show how this is possible, Todes points out that practical perception takes place in three stages:

> (1) In the first stage we prepare our self to perceive an object by getting into a proper position or attitude in respect to it.
> (2) Having prepared our self to perceive it, we next ready the object to be perceived. This is done by 'getting at' the object in some essentially preliminary, tentative, and easily reversible way which allows us to test, with comparatively light consequences, the desirability of going on to fully perceive the object.
> (3) In the third stage we finally perceive the object (p. 273).[23]

When we inhibit stage three, Todes claims, we transform practical perception so as to produce sensuous abstractions. 'In . . .

---

[23] Samuel J. Todes, 'The Abstract Sense of Reality' in James M. Edie, *New Essays in Phenomenology* (Chicago, Quadrangle Books, 1969) pp. 19, 20. Reprinted as Appendix II in *Body and World*.

cases of skillfully inhibited perception . . . one becomes aware of *qualities* rather than things' (p. 274).

Thus, the contemplative subject no longer experiences perceptual objects through their integrated aspects, but rather experiences collections of qualities. But, since he still experiences himself as in the world, the spectator still experiences objects in a shared context with other objects, and so as *stable* collections of *stable* qualities.[24] Such objects and qualities are precisely the reidentifiable elements required by thought.

In the spectatorial attitude, if I come across the same quality in several objects I can reidentify it as the one I saw before. It is as if one held a painter's colour chart up to Merleau-Ponty's woolly-blue carpet and found that the carpet's colour matched colour chip #29, that was not woolly at all, and, indeed, also matched the tangy-blue of blue berries and the icy-blue of ice. But such conceptual content is still not in what John McDowell calls the space of reasons.

To think about objects, requires more than simply being able to reidentify their properties. Much of our thinking concerns *possible* objects in *possible* situations that need never in fact occur. So Todes next explains how our imagination enables us to understand the products of spectatorial decomposition as *possible* objects with *possible* properties. Once we contemplate an object so that our unified and unifying body is no longer involved, our imagination enables us to conjure up the object in various possible contexts, and to imagine the qualities we have disengaged as the qualities of other possible objects. That is, we can imagine the object we are contemplating as a *type* of object that could be encountered and reidentified on other occasions, and we can conceive of it as having a set of reidentifiable features each of which could be a feature of other objects.[25]

---

[24] If the spectator were to assume an even more detached attitude, from outside the world, so to speak, as an impressionist painter does, the object would be isolated from the context it shares with other objects. Then, the object's qualities would lose their perceptual constancy. What one would then see is captured by Monet's paintings of the Rouen cathedral at various times of day. The painter shows how the cathedral's purely spectatorially perceived colour-qualities change with changes in the colour of the illumination.

[25] Such imaginative representations, nonetheless, depend on our embodied involvement. For

> only by reference to a character-of-this-world, as distinct from objects-in-this-world, can we have any ground for holding such imaginative verbal beliefs about, or undertaking such imaginative purposive action in respect to objects not in our perceptual field. For such long-range suppositions and purposes pre-suppose that the concrete as well as

Thanks to our disengagement and our imagination, the object of perception is transformed from an *actually existing* object into a *possible* object about which we can form hypotheses and, on the basis of which, we can make inferences, i.e. we have turned the perceptual object into an object of thought. And, just as when we abandon absorbed coping and act attentively, it seems that we have been trying to achieve a goal all along, and, when we make our needs determinate by satisfying them, we seem to have had those determinate needs all along, so, when we abandon practical perception for the detached, imaginative attitude in which we think and do philosophy, it seems that the objects of practical perception must have been objects of thought all along.

Once the stages by which the body turns the objects of practical perception into the objects of thought has been covered up by detached philosophical reflection, McDowell, like Kant, can conceive of only two alternatives: either perception is so radically non-conceptual as to be totally outside the space of reasons and, therefore, blind, or, if it is to enable us to form beliefs and make inferences, it must be as conceptual as thought itself. McDowell, therefore, can understand perception as the result of a causal, mechanical interaction of the physical body and the world, but he holds that what one passively receives in perception must be directly available for forming judgments and so must be permeated by conceptual content. There is no place in such a view for the body's motor intentionality and for the perceptual objects that it reveals. But, as we have now seen, Todes shows how, thanks to our bodily dispositions, perceptual objects are articulated without being *conceptually* articulated. Conception is then accomplished by means of a detached, spectatorial perception that can transform these articulations into decontextualized qualities, so that these qualities, in turn, can be represented as possible features of possible objects by the imagination, and thus serve as material for conceptual thought.

> formal kinds of order self-evidently manifest to us within our perceptual field (in virtue of our centrally habit-forming active body), generally hold also in the apparently placeless regions beyond our perceptual horizon – merely in virtue of the fact that these regions are also regions in the same world as the perceptually present region. (135)

This important qualification is part of Todes's argument that, although neither of the two modes of intelligibility he distinguishes can be reduced to the other, embodied perception is more basic than disembodied thought. I cannot, however, deal with this important issue within the space of this essay.

Todes concludes:

> Phenomenological analyses have shown that perception and imagination are radically different. We have two irreducibly *different* ways of experiencing things; by anticipating them; and by immediate production of them. Neither capacity is derivable from the other. Yet we are not bound to understand one in terms of the other. We can pass back and forth between them as modes of understanding (p. 201).

Conclusion

We have seen that the embodied subject is able to meet its needs by developing more and more refined skills for coping with the various determinable objects that show up in its spatio-temporal field. We have also seen that the perceiver's non-conceptual readiness to cope with the world and the things in it exhibits the perceptual equivalents of belief, inference and judgment. Finally we have seen that, for ongoing coping to take place at all, it must be continually succeeding in getting a grip on its object. Todes, therefore, claims that the perceiver has *practical objective knowledge* of the world and the objects in it. He sums up this crucial claim as follows:

> We perceive always *that* something is so. 'I see a chair', implies 'I see that there is a chair' . . . Perceptual determinations make sense only in the context of a judgment (p. 217).

This may sound at first like a concession to Stroud's claim that perceiving is judging and therefore not purely receptive, as well as a concession to McDowell's claim that, in order to enter the space of reasons, perception must be receptive yet somehow conceptual, but, we must remember that, for Todes, *perceptual* knowledge is not decontextualized knowledge. It is the result of a specific movement from need to satisfaction. Successfully coping with an object, perceptually 'justifies' the perceptual 'judgment that' there is, in fact, an object that satisfies and retroactively makes determinate the need that motivated the coping. For example, as I enter my office, I 'judge' that coping with this, as yet indeterminate object, as my chair will give me a grip on my circumstances. That is, I'm set to exercise my specific skill for sitting on this chair in these circumstances. 'I perceive that there is a chair', means, where practical perception is concerned, that my set to cope with the chair by sitting on it is successful.

Todes sums up as follows:

A perceptual judgement is an argument. . . . We have . . . found the primary form of this argument. It is a three-stage motivational argument: from our ineluctable unity of need which prompts all our activity, through our consequent finding of some unity of object, to a concluding unity of satisfaction derived from this object. All perceptual sense makes sense in the context of this argument (p. 217).

References

Dreyfus, Hubert, L. (2000). 'A Merleau-Pontian Critique of Husserl's and Searle's Representationalist Accounts of Action', *Proceedings of the Aristotelian Society*.

Embree, Lester, E. (1972) 'Biographical Sketch', in *Life-World and Consciousness: Essays for Aron Gurwitsch* (Northwestern University Press).

Gurwitsch, Aron. (1964). *The Field of Consciousness* (Duquesne University Press).

Kelly, Sean, D. (1999). 'What do we see (when we do)?' in *Philosophical Topics*, vol. 27, no. 2.

Kelly, Sean, D. (2001). 'Demonstrative concepts and experience', *Philosophical Review*, Vol. 110, No. 3.

Kelly, Sean, D. (2001). 'The non-conceptual content of perceptual experience: situation dependence and fineness of grain', *Philosophy and Phenomenological Research* (with response by Christopher Peacocke), vol. LXII, no. 3.

McDowell, John. (1994). *Mind and World* (Harvard University Press).

Merleau-Ponty, Maurice. (1945). *Phénoménologie de la perception* (Paris: Éditions Gallimard. Translation: (1962). *Phenomenology of Perception*. C. Smith, trans. (London: Routledge & Kegan Paul).

Merleau-Ponty, Maurice. (1964). 'The Film and the New Psychology', in *Sense and Non-sense*, trans. Hubert L. Dreyfus and Patricia Allen Dreyfus, (Chicago: Northwestern University Press).

Searle, John R. (1983). *Intentionality* (Cambridge: Cambridge University Press).

Sheets-Johnstone, Maxine. (1990). *The Roots of Thinking*, (Temple University Press).

Todes, Samuel J. (1969). 'The Abstract Sense of Reality', in James M. Edie, *New Essays in Phenomenology* (Chicago: Quadrangle Books). Reprinted as Appendix II in *Body and World*.

Todes, Samuel. (2001). *Body and World* (MIT Press).

Varela, F. J., Thompson, E. & Rosch, E. (1991). *The embodied mind: Cognitive science and human experience* (MIT Press).

6

LIVED BODY vs GENDER:
REFLECTIONS ON SOCIAL STRUCTURE AND
SUBJECTIVITY

Iris Marion Young

In her thorough and provocative essay, 'What Is a Woman?' Toril Moi argues that recent feminist and queer theorizing has brought us to the end of a constructivist gender rope.[1] While feminist theory of the 1970's found a distinction between sex and gender liberating both for theory and practice, subsequent feminist and queer critiques have rightly questioned the distinction. By destabilizing categories both of biological sex and gender identity, recent deconstructive approaches to feminist and queer theorizing have opened greater possibilities for thinking a plurality of intersecting identities and practices. Deconstructive challenge to the sex/gender distinction has increasingly abstracted from embodiment, however, at the same time that it has rendered a concept of gender virtually useless for theorizing subjectivity and identity. At this theoretical pass, Moi proposes that we throw over the concept of gender altogether and renew a concept of the lived body derived from existential phenomenology, as a means of theorizing sexual subjectivity without danger either of biological reductionism or gender essentialism.

Moi is not alone in proposing that feminist and queer theory question the usefulness of a concept of gender even more deeply than have deconstructive critiques, and I will refer to other recent writings that make similar points in the course of my discussion. I concentrate on Moi because her analysis of the evolution of our troubles with gender is so thorough, and because I find attractive her proposal that feminist and queer theory adopt a concept of the lived body to do the work that she argues that the category of gender does not do well. I find Moi's argument incomplete, however. While she is correct that gender is a problematic concept for theorizing subjectivity, there are or ought to be other aspects of feminist and queer theorizing that

[1] Toril Moi, 'What is a Woman?', in *What is a Woman and Other Essays* (Oxford: Oxford University Press, 2001).

cannot do without a concept of gender. By reflecting on Moi's account of recent feminist and queer theorizing, we discover that these aspects, which concern social structure more than subjectivity and identity, have been relatively neglected. The oppression of women and people who transgress heterosexual norms occurs through systemic processes and social structures which need description that uses different concepts from those appropriate for describing subjects and their experience. Moi's proposal to reconstitute a concept of the lived body helps for the latter, but for the former we need a reconstituted concept of gender.

I. The sex-gender distinction

Early feminist appropriations of what until then had been an obscure psychological distinction between gender, as referring to self-conception and behaviour, and sex, as referring to anatomy and physiology, were very theoretically and politically productive. At this theoretical moment challenging the conviction that 'biology is destiny' was an important feminist project. In order to argue for opening wider opportunities for women, we needed ways to conceptualize capacities and dispositions of members of both sexes that distanced behaviour, temperament, and achievement from biological or natural explanations. A distinction between sex and gender served this purpose. Feminists could affirm that of course men and women are 'different' in physique and reproductive function, while denying that these differences have any relevance for the opportunities members of the sexes should have or the activities that they should engage in. Such gender rules and expectations are socially constituted and socially changeable. Much of this early second wave feminist theorizing invoked an ideal of equality for women that envisioned an end to gender. 'Androgyny' named the ideal that many feminists theorized, a social condition in which biological sex would have no implications for a person's life prospects, or the way people treated one another (including, importantly, in the most consistent of these theories, one's choice of sex partners). These androgynous persons in the transformed liberated society would have no categorically distinct forms of dress, comportment, occupations, propensities toward aggression or passivity, associated with their embodiment. We would all be just people with various bodies.[2]

[2] For one statement of the androgynous ideal, see Ann Ferguson, 'Androgyny as an Ideal for Human Development', in *Sexual Democracy: Women, Oppression and Revolution* (Westview: Allen and Unwin, 1991).

This appeal to an ideal of androgyny was short lived. Some of the turning point texts of feminist theory in the late 1970's and early 1980's turned instead to accounts of the social and psychological specificities of femininely gendered identity and social perspective derived from gender roles. While not at all explained by biological distinctions between men and women, nevertheless there are deep social divisions of masculine and feminine gendered dispositions and experience which have implications for the psychic lives of men and women, their interactions with one another, their dispositions to care for children or exercise authority. Nancy Chodorow, Carol Gilligan, Nancy Hartsock and others developed theories of feminine gender identities as expressing a general structure of subjectivity and social standpoint in significant ways defining the lives and possibilities of most women.[3]

No sooner had such a general account of feminine gender identity emerged than it came under attack as 'essentialist'. These accounts assume mothering as defining the experience of most women. They fail to inquire about the differences that race or class positioning make to caring practices, and they assume that women are or wish to be in relationships with men. They extrapolate from the historical specificity of twentieth century affluent urban nuclear families and occupations structures, ignoring historical and cross-cultural specifications in the organization of family and work. Although the criticisms were not always voiced in the fairest way, most feminist theorists took their points to heart.

Queer theory broke into this dissolution of gender theory, in the person of writers such as Diana Fuss and Judith Butler. Because Moi focuses on Butler's subversion of the sex-gender distinction, and I will support Moi's conclusion in specific respects, I will follow Moi in this focus.

In *Gender Trouble*, Butler questioned the motive of feminist theory to seek a theory of gender identity. Feminists believe they need such a general theory of gender, she argued, in order to know what is the subject of feminist politics. Feminism has no meaning as a specific transformative social movement, it is thought, without an account of the 'agent' of change, the subject

---

[3] Nancy Chodorow, *The Reproduction of Mothering* (Berkeley: University of California Press, 1978; 2n edition 1999); Carol Gilligan, *In a Different Voice* (Cambridge: Harvard University Press, 1982); Nancy C. M. Hartsock, *Money, Sex and Power: Toward a Feminist Historical Materialism* (Notheastern University Press, 1983).

to be liberated; that subject is 'woman', and 'gender' is the concept that displays what a woman is. As gendered, 'women' are distinct from the biological sex, female. Butler argued, however, that the feminist distinction between sex and gender nevertheless retains a binarism of stable categorical complementarity between male and female, which reproduces a logic of heterosexual normativity. The very distinction between sex and gender ought to be put in question in order to challenge any reliance on a distinction between nature and culture, or any conception that subjects have inner lives to which an idea of stable gender identity corresponds. Gender is nothing other than a social performative. The discursive rules of normative heterosexuality produce gendered performances that subjects reiterate and cite; the sexing of bodies themselves derives from such performatives. In this process of reiterated gender performance some persons become constituted as abject, outside the heterosexual binary. Radical politics, then, consists in troubling the gender binaries and playing with gender citation.

In response to the critical reaction of some commentators that her theory of gender as performance makes bodies and sexual identity simply a product of discourse, in *Bodies That Matter* Butler argues that the materiality of sexed bodies is itself socially constituted. She insists that such production of bodies is not 'idealist', and that a valuation of 'materialism' over 'idealism' itself relies on a questionable binary logic.

Moi does not refute Butler's arguments, which she takes to be cogent, given their terms and methods. She argues nevertheless that ideals of subjectivity and sexuality have become increasingly abstract in this train of theorizing that begins with the sex-gender distinction and ends deconstructing a material-ideal dichotomy. It is not clear at this point what lived problems the theory addresses or how the concepts help people understand and describe their experience. Butler successfully calls into question the logic of the sex-gender distinction, yet her theorizing never goes beyond these terms and remains tied to them. This line of critique, Moi argues, calls for throwing off the idea of gender altogether as useful for understanding subjectivity and identity. Queer theory and practice bend gender meanings, aiming to loosen them from the normative polarities of hegemonic masculinity and femininity. Moi suggests that queer and feminist theorists should make a break with gender altogether.

II. The lived body

For an alternative to the categories of sex and gender, Moi proposes to return to the framework of existential phenomenology on which Simone de Beauvoir relies.[4] The central category for this theoretical approach is that of the *lived body*. A reconstituted concept of the lived body, Moi argues, would offer feminists an idea that can serve the function we have wanted from the sex-gender categorization, without bringing its problems.

The lived body is a unified idea of a physical body acting and experiencing in a specific socio-cultural context; it is body-in-situation. For existentialist theory, *situation* denotes the produce of *facticity* and *freedom*. The person always faces the material facts of her body and its relation to a given environment. Her bodily organs have certain feeling capacities and function in determinate ways; her size, age, health and training make her capable of strength and movement in relation to her environment in specific ways. Her skin has a particular colour, her face determinate features, her hair particular colour and texture, each with their own aesthetic properties. Her specific body lives in a specific context – crowded by other people, anchored to the earth by gravity, surrounded by buildings and streets with a unique history, hearing particular languages, having food and shelter available, or not, as a result of culturally specific social processes that make specific requirements on her to access them. All these concrete material relations of a person's bodily existence and her physical and social environment constitute her *facticity*.

The person, however, is an actor; she has an ontological freedom to construct herself in relation to this facticity. The human actor has specific projects, things she aims to accomplish, ways she aims to express herself, make her mark on the world, transform

---

[4] Sonia Kruks gives a reading of the existentialism of Simone de Beauvoir that aims to respond to contemporary conundrums of 'identity politics' in feminist theory. She too proposes to understand Beauvoir as developing a concept of the lived body useful for feminist theory, and she argues that interpretations of Beauvoir have failed to appreciate the extent to which she was influenced by Maurice Merleau-Ponty's concept of the lived body; see Kruks, 'Freedoms that Matter: Subjectivity and Situation in the Work of Beauvoir, Sartre and Merleau-Ponty', in Kruks, *Retrieving Experience: Subjectivity and Recognition in Feminist Politics* (Ithaca: Cornell University Press, 2001), pp. 27–51. Debra B. Bergoffen also recommends a return to Simone de Beauvoir as a way out of conundrums of gender theorizing to which recent feminist and queer theories have come. See Bergoffen, 'Simone de Beauvoir: Disrupting the Metonymy of Gender', in Dorothea Olkowski, ed., *Resistance, Flight, Creation: Feminist Enactments of French Philosophy* (Ithaca: Cornell University Press, 2000), pp. 97–119.

her surroundings and relationships. Often these are projects she engages in jointly with others. *Situation*, then, is the way that the facts of embodiment, social and physical environment appear in light of the projects a person has. She finds that her movements are awkward in relation to her desire to dance. She sees the huge city with its thousand year history as an opportunity for learning about her ancestors. 'To claim that the body is a situation is to acknowledge that the meaning of a woman's body is bound up with the way she uses her freedom' (Moi, p. 65).

How does Moi propose that the idea of the lived body might replace that of gender, and the distinction between sex and gender? Like the category of sex, that of the lived body can refer to the specific physical facts of bodies, including sexual and reproductive differentiation. 'Woman' and 'man' name the physical facticity of certain bodies, some with penises, others with clitorises and breasts, each with differing experiences of desire and sexual feeling. A category of lived body, moreover, need not make sexual difference dimorphous; some bodies have physical traits like those of men in certain respects and those of women in others. People experience their desires and feeling in diverse ways that do not neatly correlate with sexual dimorphism or heterosexual norms. As a lived body, moreover, perceptual capacities and motility are not distinct from association with sexual specificity; nor is size, bone structure or skin colour. Most important for the proposal Moi makes, the concept of the lived body, unlike the concept of sex, is not biologistic. It does not refer to an objectivist scientific account that generalizes laws of physiology and function. A scientific approach to bodies proceeds at a significantly higher level of abstraction than does a description of bodies as lived. The idea of the lived body thus can bring the physical facts of different bodies into theory without the reductionist and dichotomous implications of the category of 'sex'.

The idea of the lived body, moreover, refuses the distinction between nature and culture that grounds a distinction between sex and gender. The body as lived is always enculturated: by the phonemes a body learns to pronounce at a very early age, by the clothes the person wears that mark her nation, her age, her occupational status, and in what is culturally expected or required of women. The body is enculturated by habits of comportment distinctive to interactional settings of business or pleasure; often they are specific to locale or group. Contexts of discourse and interaction position persons in systems of evaluation and expectations which often implicate their embodied being; the person experiences herself as looked at in certain ways, described in her physical being in certain ways, she experiences the bodily reactions of others to her, and she reacts to them. The diverse phenomena that have come under the rubric of 'gender' in feminist theory can be redescribed in the idea of lived body as some among many forms of bodily habitus and interactions with others that we enact and experience. In such redescription we find that Butler is right in at least this respect: it is a mystification to attribute the ways of being associated with the category 'gender' to some inner core of identity of a subject, whether understood as 'natural' or acquired.

In a recent essay Linda Nicholson similarly proposes that feminist and queer theory focus on the socio-historically differentiation of bodies as lived, rather then maintain a distinction between biological sex and embodiment and gender as historically variable. To the extent that this distinction between sex and gender remains, feminist theory continues a 'biological foundationalism', as distinct from biological reductionism. The study of sexuality, reproduction and the roles assigned to men and women should consist in reading bodies themselves and not presume a nature/culture distinction that considers gender as 'merely cultural'.[5]

The idea of the lived body thus does the work the category 'gender' has done, but better and more. It does this work better because the category of the lived body allows description of the habits and interactions of men with women, women with women, and men with men in ways that can attend to the plural possibilities of comportment, without necessary reduction to the normative heterosexual binary of 'masculine' and 'feminine'. It does more because it helps avoid a problem generated by use of ascriptive general categories such as 'gender,' 'race,' 'nationality,' 'sexual orientation', to describe the constructed identities of individuals, namely the additive character that identities appear to have under this description. If we conceptualize individual identities as constituted by the diverse group identities – gender, race, class, sexual orientation, and so on – there seems to be a mystery both about how persons are individualized, and how these different group identities combine in the person. With the idea of the lived body there is no such puzzle. Each person is a distinctive

---

[5] Linda Nicholson, 'Interpreting Gender', *The Play of Reason: From the Modern to the Postmodern* (Ithaca: Cornell University Press, 1999), pp. 53–76.

body, with specific features, capacities, and desires, that are similar to and different from those of others in determinate respects.
She is born in a particular place and time, is raised in a particular
family setting, and all these have specific socio-cultural histories
that stand in relation to the history of others in particular ways.
What we call categories of gender, race, ethnicity, etc. are short
hand for a set of structures that position persons, a point to which
I will return. They are not properly theorized as general group
identities that add together to constitute individual identities.
The individual person lives out her unique body in a socio-historical context of the behaviour and expectations of others, but she
does not have to worry about constituting her identity from a set
of generalized 'pop-beads' strung together.[6]

By means of a category of the lived body, then, 'One can arrive
at a highly historicized and concrete understanding of bodies and
subjectivity without relying on the sex-gender distinction that
Butler takes as axiomatic' (Nicholson 1999, p. 46). The idea of
the lived body recognizes that a person's subjectivity is condi-
tioned by socio-cultural facts and the behaviour and expectations
of others in ways that she has not chosen. At the same time, the
theory of the lived body says that each person takes up and acts in
relation to these unchosen facts in her own way.

> To consider the body as a situation . . . is to consider both the
> fact of being a specific kind of body and the meaning that
> concrete body has for the situated individual. This is not the
> equivalent of either sex or gender. The same is true for 'lived
> experience' which encompasses our experience of all kinds of
> situations (race, class, nationality, etc.) and is a far more wide-
> ranging concept than the highly psychologizing concept of
> gender identity (Nicholson 1999, p. 81).

III. Is the lived body enough?

Toril Moi argues that a concept of the lived body serves feminist
theoretical purposes better than a concept of gender. She
defines those purposes as providing a theory of subjectivity and
the body, and providing an understanding of what it means to
be a woman or man in a particular society (pp. 4, 36, 14).
Feminist theory, she says, ought to become a project of

---

[6] See Elizabeth Spelman, *Inessential Woman: Problems of Exclusion in Feminist Thought*
(Boston: Beacon Press, 1988).

dispelling confusions concerning bodies, sex, sexuality, sexual difference, and the power relations among women and men, heterosexuals and homosexuals (p. 120). This last phrase about power relations is extremely vague. Depending on how it is specified, the scope of theorizing power relations might fall beyond what I take as Moi's major emphasis in defining the tasks of feminist theory. She defines this theory as focusing on subjectivity, who one is as an agent, the attributes and capacities one has for experience, the relations with others that contribute to one's sense of self. In the essay I referred to earlier, Linda Nicholson also seems to consider that the theoretical function that a concept of gender has meant to serve is that of theorizing self-identity and the social constitution of the human character.

Recent discussions questioning the stability of gender and the adequacy of a sex-gender distinction reveal dilemmas and increasing abstraction into which feminist and queer theory has either been forced or has had to respond to. These problems with a concept of gender have surfaced at least partly because gender aims to be a general category, but subjectivity is always particular. Moi's appropriation of the concept of the lived body offers more refined tools for theorizing sexed subjectivity, and the experience of differently situated men and women than does the more blunt category of gender. Agreeing with this means dispensing with gender altogether, however, only if the projects of feminist and queer theories consist only in theorizing subjectivity. But I think they are not. The debates about gender and essentialism that Moi aims to bring to a close with her arguments have, I think, tended to narrow the interests of feminists and queer theorists to issues of experience, identity and subjectivity. Her discussion clears the way for asking whether other aspects of a project for feminist and queer theory have been obscured by these debates, for which a resituated concept of gender might still be needed. In the remaining pages of this essay I want to suggest that a concept of gender is important for theorizing social structures and their implications for the freedom and well being of persons.

As I understand them, feminist and queer theory consist not only in giving account of the meaning of the lives of women and men in all their relational and sexual diversity. Nor is it only about analyzing how discourses construct subjects and the stereotypical or defamatory aspects of some of these discourses that contribute to the suffering of some men and women who fall on the wrong

side of normalizing processes. Feminist and queer theories are
also projects of social criticism. These are theoretical efforts to
identify certain wrongful harms or injustices, locate and explain
their sources in institutions and social relations, and propose
directions for institutionally oriented action to change them. This
latter set of tasks requires the theorist to have an account not only
of individual experience, subjectivity, and identity, but also of
social structures.

In other writings I have articulated a concept of social structure
specifically directed at the project of giving institutional account
of sources of injustice and in response to the dilemmas that
emerge from claiming that individuals share group identities.[7]
Structures denote the confluence of institutional rules and interactive routines, mobilization of resources, and physical structures,
which constitute the historical givens in relation to which individuals act, and which are relatively stable over time. Structures also
connote the wider social outcomes that result from the confluence of many individual actions within given institutional relations, whose collective consequences often do not bear the mark
of any person or group's intention.

Alexander Wendt distinguishes two levels or kinds of structure,
micro and macro levels. Micro structures refer to structural analysis of interaction. The patterning of practices and interactive
routines, the rules which actors implicitly or explicitly follow and
the resources and instruments they mobilize in their interactions
can all be regarded as structured. Gender structures are very
important to interactions at this micro level. In recommending
that feminist social theory complement attention to subjectivity
and identity with renewed attention to social structures, however,
I am more concerned with what Wendt refers to as the macro
level, which involve 'multiply realizable outcomes'.[8] That is to say,
social theory that wishes to understand and criticize the
constraints on individuals and groups that render them relatively
unfree and limited in their opportunities in relation to others
need to have a picture of large-scale systemic outcomes of the

---

[7] See *Inclusion and Democracy* (Oxford: Oxford University Press, 2000), especially
Chapter 3; see also 'Equality of Whom? Social Groups and Judgments of Injustice', *Journal
of Political Philosophy*, Vol. 9, no. 1, March 2001, pp. 1–18. There I build a definition of
social structures by drawing primarily on ideas of Peter Blau, Anthony Giddens and Jean
Paul Sartre.

[8] Alexander Wendt, *Social Theory and International Relations* (Cambridge: Cambridge
University Press, 2000), Chapter 4.

operations of many institutions and practices which produce outcomes that constrain some people in specific ways at the same time that they enable others. Macro structures depend on micro-level interactions for their production and reproduction, according to Wendt, but their form and the ways they constrain and enable cannot be reduced to effects of particular interactions.

Social structures position individuals in relations of labour and production, power and subordination, desire and sexuality, prestige and status. The way a person is positioned in structures is as much a function of how other people treat him or her within various institutional settings as it is the attitude a person takes to himself or herself. Any individual occupies multiple positions in structure, and these positionings become differently salient depending on the institutional setting and the position of others there.

From the point of view of critical social theory, the main reason to care about structures is in order to have an account of the constitution and causes of social inequality. Some people encounter relative constraints in their freedom and material well being as the cumulative effect of the possibilities of their social positions, as compared with others who in their social positions have more options or easier access to benefits. Social groups defined by caste, class, race, age, ethnicity, and, of course, gender, name subjective identities less than axes of such structural inequality. They name structural positions whose occupants are privileged or disadvantaged in relation to one another due to the adherence of actors to institutional rules and norms and the pursuit of their interests and goals within institutions. A structural account offers a way of understanding inequality of opportunity, oppression and domination, that does not seek individualized perpetrators, but rather considers most actors complicit in its production, to a greater or lesser degree.

Nancy Folbre conceptualizes such issues of social inequality in terms she calls 'structures of constraint.'[9] Structures of constraint include sets of asset distributions, rules, norms and preferences that afford more freedom and opportunity for benefits to some than others. Constraints define the range of options available to individuals, or the costs of pursuing some options rather than others. Time and money are basic assets. Legal rules function as important constraints, but so do cultural norms. They impose a

[9] Nancy Folbre, *Who Pays for the Kids?* (New York: Routledge, 1994), especially Chapter 2.

'price' on nonconformity. Preferences can be constraints when they conflict with one another. A configuration of particular assets, rules, norms and preferences creates the constraints that define what we call social groups based on gender, class, race, age, and so on. Thus membership in the group called 'women' is the product of a loose configuration of different structural factors.

To describe and explain some of the structures and processes that produce differential opportunities and privileges in contemporary society, I suggest, we cannot do without a concept of gender. Feminist and queer theories need conceptual tools to describe the rules and practices of institutions that presume differing roles for men and women, and/or which presume that men and women are coupled with each other in intimate relations. We need tools for understanding how and why certain patterns in the allocation of tasks or status recognition remain persistent in ways that limit the options of many women and of most people whose sexual and intimate choices deviate from heterosexual norms. An important conceptual shift occurs, however, when we understand the concept of gender as a tool for theorizing structures more than subjects. We no longer need to ascribe a single or shared gender identity to men and women.

My own effort to respond to critiques of early feminist theories of gender turned in this direction of theorizing gender as an attribute of social structures more than of persons. In 'Gender as Seriality: Thinking About Women as a Social Collective,' I draw on a concept from Sartre's later philosophy, his idea of a series.[10] Gender, I suggest there, is best understood as a particular form of the social positioning of lived bodies in relation to one another within historically and socially specific institutions and processes that have material effects on the environment in which people act and reproduce relations of power and privilege among them. On this account, what it means to say that individual persons are 'gendered' is that we all *find ourselves* passively grouped according to these structural relations, in ways too impersonal to ground identity. There I proposed that there are two basic axes of gender structures: a sexual division of labour and normative heterosexuality. Here I will take a lead from Bob Connell and add to these a third axis, gendered hierarchies of power.[11]

---

[10] In I.M. Young, *Intersecting Voices: Dilemmas of Gender, Political Philosophy and Policy* (Princeton: Princeton University Press, 1997).

[11] R. W. Connell, *Gender and Power* (Stanford: Stanford University Press, 1987).

The structuring of work and occupations by gender is a basic aspect of all modern societies (and many premodern societies), with far reaching consequences for the lives of individuals, the constraints and opportunities they face. The core of a gendered division of labour in modern societies is the division between 'private' and 'public' work. An aspect of the basic structure of these societies is that the work of caring – for persons, their bodily needs, their emotional well being, and the maintenance of their dwellings – takes place primarily in unpaid labour in private homes. While recent decades have seen some changes in the allocation of this work between men and women, it is still the case that this unpaid caring and household work falls primarily to women. The operations of the entire society depend on the regular performance of this work, yet it goes relatively unnoticed and little valued. The persons to whom this work is assigned have less time and energy to devote to other tasks and activities than do those who do less of it. This gendered division of labour persists apparently because people collectively do not wish to organize broadly funded public services that take more collective responsibility for care work. Despite many significant changes in gender ideas and ideology in contemporary societies, there has been little change in this basic division of labour. Indeed, neo-liberal economic policies across the globe have had the effect of retrenching this division where it may have loosened.

Feminist social and political theory in the last twenty years has documented dozens of ways that this gendered structure constrains the opportunities of those persons doing unpaid care work, mostly women.[12] They work longer hours than others, and are rendered dependent on other people for provision of their needs, which makes them vulnerable to poverty or abuse. Feminist researchers have also documented how this basic structure underlies occupational divisions in public paid work according to gender. When occupations involve caring they tend to become female gendered. Because many women arrange their public work lives in relation to caring responsibilities, only a relatively small number of occupations welcome them, which helps keep wages low in those occupations. The structuring of both private and public work along these lines exhibits gendered hierarchies of status and power, not to mention financial reward.

---

[12] Nancy Folbre's book, cited above, is an excellent analysis of the operations of these constraints in several countries in Europe, Asia and Latin America as well as the United States.

It might be thought that these structural consequences of a sexual division of labour describe Western industrial societies primarily. Theorized at the right level of categorical generality, however, similar structures describe much about many less developed countries, especially in urban life. As some feminist scholars of development have argued, for example, both government policy and the policies of international organizations such as the International Monetary Fund implicitly rely on the assumption that unpaid domestic labour is infinitely expandable, and that household caretakers are available to take up the slack in meeting the needs of their family members when food subsidies are slashed, school fees go up, or health clinics are closed.

A structural account of the sexual division of labour, that is, does not assume that this division of labour has the same content across societies. It is a theoretical framework that asks whether there are tasks and occupations usually performed by members of one sex or the other, and/or whether the social norms and cultural products of the society tend to represent certain tasks or occupations as more appropriately performed by members of one sex or the other. For any society, both today and in the past, the answer is usually yes, but there is nevertheless considerable variation among them in *which* occupations are sex associated, the ideologies often legitimating these associations, how many tasks are sex typed, and what implications this sexual division of labour has for the distribution of resources among persons, their relative status, and the constraints and opportunities that condition their lives.

A second axis of gender structuring in our society is normative heterosexuality. This structuring consists in the diverse institutional and ideological facts that privilege heterosexual coupling. These include the form and implications of many legal institutions, many rules and policies of private organizations in allocating positions and benefits, the structuring of schooling and mainstream media to accord with these institutions, as well as the assumptions many people make in their everyday interactions with others. Together such social facts make structures with differential consequences on the lives of different men and women, and which sometimes produce serious suffering or wrongful limitations on freedom. The system of normative heterosexuality significantly constrains the lives of men and women, with all their varying sexual and desiring inclinations, motivating some to adjust their lives in ways they believe will bring them material

reward and acceptance, and others to carve out lives in the inter-
stices of social relations where their desires and projects do not
fit, or openly rebel.

Cheshire Calhoun argues that lesbian and gay subordination
is different in form from the structural constraints on the lives of
women or people of colour, for example. Whereas structures of
female subordination or institutionalized racism confine people
perceived as belonging to certain categories as having certain
places or positions, Calhoun argues that persons who transgress
heterosexual norms have no legitimized place at all in political
citizenship, civil society, or private spheres. Structures of normative heterosexuality constrain lesbians and gay men by enforcing
their invisibility.[13]

An institutionalized valuation of particular associations of
maleness or masculinity condition hierarchies of power in ways
that constrain the possible actions of many people seem quite
resistant to change. Positions and practices of institutionalized
and organized violence are most important here – military and
police forces, prison systems, etc. In general, the structuring of
state institutions, corporations and other bureaucracies according to hierarchies of decision making authority and status afford
some people significant privileges and freedom, and these are
usually men, at the same time that they limit, constrain and subordinate others, including most women and many men. Gendered
hierarchies of power intersect with a sexual division of labour and
normative heterosexuality in many ways to reproduce a sense of
entitlement of men to women's service and an association of
heterosexual masculinity with force and command.

When describing social structures as gendered it is neither
necessary to make generalizations about men and women nor is
it necessary to reduce varying gender structures to a common
principle. A gendered occupational division of labour may
strongly code certain occupations as female and others as male,
and these codings may have far reaching implications for the
power, prestige and material reward incumbents of each enjoy.
Nothing follows from this, however, about what most men or most
women do for a living. Recognizing the structures of normative
heterosexuality may well result in theorizing plural understandings of gender, varying rules and practices that make expectations

---

[13] Cheshire Calhoun, *Feminism, the Family, and the Politics of the Closet: Lesbian and Gay Displacement* (Oxford: Oxford University Press, 2000).

on men and women regarding sexual interaction, relation of adults and children, social aesthetics, relationship of persons to workplace roles, and so on, that do not share a common logic and in some respects may be in tension with one another. Structures of a gendered hierarchy of power differentiate men from one another according to social roles and dispositions, and do not simply differentiate men and women. The most important thing about the analysis is to understand how the rules, relations and their material consequences produce privileges for some people that underlie an interest in their maintenance, at the same time that they limit options of others, cause relative deprivations in their lives, or render them vulnerable to domination and exploitation.

In this essay I have agreed with Toril Moi's proposal that the existential phenomenological category of the lived body is a richer and more flexible concept than gender for theorizing the socially constituted experience of women and men than either concepts of sex or gender. The lived body is particular in its morphology, material similarities and differences from other bodies. I have argued, moreover, that this proposal should not mean dispensing with a category of gender, but rather confining its use to analysis of social structures for the purposes of understanding certain specific relations of power, opportunity and resource distribution. An obvious question arises at this point, as to the relation of lived bodies to these structures.

Another reason that turning to a concept of lived body may be productive for feminist and queer theory is precisely that it can offer a way of articulating how persons live out their positioning in social structures along with the opportunities and constraints they produce. I do not have the space here to develop the framework for such articulation, and I will offer only a few lines toward a sketch.

Gender structures, I said above, are historically given and condition the action and consciousness of individual persons. They precede that action and consciousness. Each person experiences aspects of gender structures as facticity, as socio-historical givens with which she or he must deal. Every person faces the question of what to wear, for example, and clothing options and conventions derive from multiple structures of profit seeking, class and occupational distinction, income distribution, heterosexual normativity, and spaces and expectations of occasions and activities and the possibilities of conformity and transgression they bring. However limited the choices or the resources to enact them, each person takes up the constrained possibilities that gender structures offer in their own way, forming their own habits as variations on those possibilities, or actively try to resist or refigure them. Gender as structured is also lived through individual bodies, always as personal experiential response and not as a set of attributes that individuals have in common

Pierre Bourdieu's concept of the *habitus* offers one interpretation of how generalized social structures are produced and reproduced in the movement and interaction of bodies. Especially in his understanding of gender structures, however, Bourdieu's understanding of the relation of social structures to actors and experience conceptualizes these structures too rigidly and ahistorically.[14] It may be more fruitful to draw on a theory of lived body like that of Maurice Merleau-Ponty, but connect it more explicitly than he does to how the body lives out its positions in social structures of the division of labour, hierarchies of power, and norms of sexuality.[15] Under the influence of such a theory of how bodies live out their structured positioning, moreover, one might find that a deconstructive gender theory such as Judith Butler's appears not as a theory of the determination or constitution of gendered subjects, but as a theory of the variable movements of habituated bodies both reacting to, reproducing, and modifying structures.

References

Bergoffen, Debra, B. (2000). 'Simone de Beauvoir: Disrupting the Metonymy of Gender', in Dorothea Olkowski, ed., *Resistance, Flight, Creation: Feminist Enactments of French Philosophy* (Ithaca: Cornell University Press).

[14] See for example, Pierre Bourdieu, *The Logic of Practice*, Richard Nice, trans., (Stanford: Stanford University Press, 1990), especially Chapters 3 and 4. Toril Moi herself explores the implications of Bourdieu's theory for feminist theory; see 'Appropriating Bourdieu: Feminist Theory and Pierre Bourdieu's Sociology of Culture,' Chapter 3 of *What is a Woman?* Bourdieu's book, *La Domination Masculine* (Paris: Editions du Seuil, 1998) assumes that he can generalize about gender structures largely from his observations of the Kabylic society in North Africa.

[15] Nick Crossley argues that a reconstruction of Merleau-Ponty's theory of sociality and habit can better serve social theory than Bourdieu's concept of *habitus* because Merleau-Ponty's conceptualization gives more place to freedom and individual difference. See Crossley, 'The Phenomenological Habitus and Its Construction,' *Theory and Society* Vol. 30, 2001, pp. 81-120; see also 'Habitus, Agency and Change: Engaging with Bourdieu,' paper presented at a conference on the Philosophy of the Social Science, Czech Academy of Sciences, Prague, May 2001.

Bourdieu, Pierre. (1990). *The Logic of Practice*, Richard Nice, trans., (Stanford: Stanford University Press).

Bourdieu, Pierre. (1998). *La Domination Masculine* (Paris: Editions du Seuil)

Calhoun, Cheshire. (2000). *Feminism, the Family, and the Politics of the Closet: Lesbian and Gay Displacement* (Oxford: Oxford University Press).

Chodorow, Nancy. (1978). *The Reproduction of Mothering* (Berkeley: University of California Press; 2nd edition 1999).

Connell, R. W. (1987). *Gender and Power* (Stanford: Stanford University Press).

Crossley, Nick. (2001). 'The Phenomenological Habitus and Its Construction,' *Theory and Society* Vol. 30, pp. 81-120.

Crossley, Nick. (2001). 'Habitus, Agency and Change: Engaging with Bourdieu,' paper presented at a conference on the Philosophy of the Social Science, Czech Academy of Sciences, Prague, May 2001.

Ferguson, Ann. (1991). 'Androgyny as an Ideal for Human Development', in *Sexual Democracy: Women, Oppression and Revolution* (Westview: Allen and Unwin).

Folbre, Nancy. (1994). *Who Pays for the Kids?* (New York: Routledge).

Gilligan, Carol. (1982). *In a Different Voice* (Cambridge: Harvard University Press).

Hartsock, Nancy, C. M. (1983). *Money, Sex and Power: Toward a Feminist Historical Materialism* (Northeastern University Press).

Kruks, Sonia. (2001). 'Freedoms that Matter: Subjectivity and Situation in the Work of Beauvoir, Sartre and Merleau-Ponty', in Kruks, *Retrieving Experience: Subjectivity and Recognition in Feminist Politics* (Ithaca: Cornell University Press).

Moi, Toril. (2001). 'Appropriating Bourdieu: Feminist Theory and Pierre Bourdieu's Sociology of Culture,' in *What is a Woman?*

Moi, Toril. (2001). 'What is a Woman?', in *What is a Woman and Other Essays* (Oxford: Oxford University Press).

Nicholson, Linda. (1999). 'Interpreting Gender', *The Play of Reason: From the Modern to the Postmodern* (Ithaca: Cornell University Press).

Spelman, Elizabeth. (1988). *Inessential Woman: Problems of Exclusion in Feminist Thought* (Boston: Beacon Press).

Wendt, Alexander. (2000). *Social Theory and International Relations* (Cambridge: Cambridge University Press).

Young, Iris, M. (1997). *Intersecting Voices: Dilemmas of Gender, Political Philosophy and Policy* (Princeton: Princeton University Press).

Young, Iris, M. (2000). *Inclusion and Democracy* (Oxford: Oxford University Press).

Young, Iris, M. (2001). 'Equality of Whom? Social Groups and Judgments of Injustice', *Journal of Political Philosophy*, Vol. 9, no. 1.

7

PSYCHOANALYSIS AND THE BODY-MIND PROBLEM

Michael Brearley

1. Introduction: Countertransference omnipotence and impotence

In this paper I want to think with you about somatic symptoms, and about the related situations in the consulting room where patients couch their communications in predominantly somatic language. A good example of the former is given by Anzieu; he describes a patient who really got up the analyst's nose with his obnoxious smell of sweat. For a long time Anzieu was unable to think of this as having any meaning, and later unable to find a way of approaching possible meaning without being offensive. He felt stuck. The other type of case is where the patient's talk remains persistently at the level of pounding heart, or stomach ache, or other bodily sensations or states.

As psychoanalysts or therapists our whole aim is towards psychological understanding, and we probably all share the incipient feeling of helplessness with such patients. It is our job to reflect on such helplessness. But at times we slide from the view of body-reports as (inevitably) difficult to understand to simply feeling inadequate. We fall into a state of paralysis in which we are unable to reflect psychoanalytically on our feelings or on the patient.

Thus we lose confidence in ourselves or in the analysis, negating our understanding of the inevitable struggle involved in moving towards knowledge, especially in such cases. One countertransference problem that such patients tend to evoke in us is the need to think we know; we may then be tempted to be wild analysts, constructing, and offering, heroic, magical and omniscient interpretations.

There are of course other possible defensive responses. We may make the error of failing to take seriously the physiological aspects and the possibility that the patient needs a medical checkup. Analysts who are also doctors may, on the other hand, revert to their former, knowing, medical standpoint, and lose touch with their analytic stance. We may, again, become moralistic and blame our patients for not offering what we want, and making our life difficult – and convey this whether directly or, more likely, subtly. By contrast we may shy away from taking seriously perverse or tricky states of mind in the patient, in which he/she utilises a thin narrative of somatic description to block psychological insights and defeat the analytic process. At such times the patient may unconsciously provoke us into omnipotent stances, which he or she can then triumphantly repudiate and disparage.

Psychoanalytic perplexity about body-mind links in relation to certain patients at certain times can merge into a more generalised, quasi-philosophical perplexity; for a philosopher may put the sceptical argument in terms of the impossibility of a purely mental event like an unconscious phantasy *ever* producing bodily changes. I will return at the end of the paper to this idea, and make some comments on the parallels and differences between philosophical doubt and pragmatic, psychoanalytic doubt over mind-body links.

In our analytic work in the consulting room, we might expect that we would not be bothered by epistemological doubts of this kind. We are concerned, one might think, with matters of fact, with what is or is not the case. On one occasion, we may have grounds for believing that particular bodily reports stand in for hidden or potential psychological and emotional meanings. Such a patient may be alexithymic, that is, unable to experience and conceive of what happens in him in emotional or articulable form (McDougall). Such a patient can't at present go further. Or, by contrast, we may suspect that, consciously or unconsciously, he or she won't go further. There may, again, be some mixture of the two. There may, for example, be a split between two parts of the self, one part operating in concrete, sensation-based evacuatory mode, with no detachment from or reflection on raw feeling, the other capable, within its comfort-zone, of symbolic thought and a more emotional level of functioning. Again, there are understandable, evidential criteria to base such understanding on, whether or not we get it right on a given occasion. Often we will not know what to believe. But however uncertain we are, we have our psychoanalytic experience and understanding to help us to be open to the patient's vibes or projections. We have an idea of what sorts of material would count as evidence, and we know that further evidence, including the patient's responses, may lead us to withdraw, revise, qualify, confirm or expand our earlier ideas. Naturally, we often don't know; but we have an idea of what it would be to know more.

Our analytic understanding should remind us, on reflection, that it is not really surprising that this is so difficult an area, because somatisation is the outcome of the subject's unconscious denial of emotional meaning, or of an incapacity to go beyond the sensory/somatic. And it is often only after we have managed to understand and tolerate our not-knowing (by what Keats called our 'negative capability') that we can begin, through careful and prolonged work with the patient, to get an often tentative idea of what these symptoms and reports might mean in more psychological terms. With such an open-minded attitude we can be particularly alert for changes in the patient's manner or speech that indicate intrusions of unconscious material, such as slips, hesitations, or the reporting of a rare dream or dream fragment (Aisenstein). We may then be able to make use of such small openings to initiate further movements in the analysis, and thus in time enable ourselves and the patient to grow towards a more fully psychic elaboration.

2. Outline

What I hope to do in this paper is consider some of the anxiety that I can feel in this area of my work. I will then mention some of the resources that psychoanalysts have discovered and developed for modifying it. I will give brief vignettes to illustrate this. I will go on to suggest that psychoanalytic theories (notably Anzieu's and Bion's) about the growth of the mind and the capacity to think show how mind emerges from what we might call body-mind; and that we are always liable to regressions to, or fixations at, earlier, bodily levels of functioning. I say something about Anzieu's idea of a 'skin ego'. Such a picture of mind counters the Cartesian view that mind and body are worlds apart (Descartes). I then give a more extended example of a struggle of my own with somatisation while writing this paper. Finally I return to the issue of philosophical or quasi-philosophical doubt in the psychoanalyst. I should add that I am not here attempting to give an account of the ways in which body experience can make a person feel alive, and can be life-enhancing.

3. Some tendencies to quasi-philosophical doubt and helplessness

The differences between conceptual (epistemological) doubt and ordinary uncertainty are not always clear-cut. Speaking for myself,

I am more likely to feel at a loss when questions about psychosomatic symptoms or illness come up. I am not troubled about everything that falls within the range of body/mind interactions. Natural expressions of emotion do not trouble me, and I can feel comfortable about the idea of hysterical symptoms. But psychosomatic events sometimes seem peculiarly puzzling. Here what I feel is akin to what Wittgenstein (1953) refers to as 'mental cramp', which, he suggests, afflicts people when they do, or begin to do, philosophy.

I will start with natural expressions of emotion, places where, as Wittgenstein also said, 'we touch rock-bottom'. We blush from embarrassment, flush with anger, go pallid when afraid, and cry from grief. Sweating, crying, blushing, shivering, mouth open, eyes wide open, panting, tachycardia, tension – all these are natural expressions of emotion. These physiological changes merge into action, doing. We strut or cower. The physiological expressions of fear merge into cringing or fleeing, those of anger into striking out, of disgust into vomiting. Fainting and becoming dizzy merge into falling asleep, which is something we can do, or try to do, or try not to do. Some patients, for example, suddenly become sleepy, or even fall asleep, at points of extreme anxiety in a session. Natural expressions of emotion are also rock-bottom for us as therapists.

Nor do I feel particular difficulty in finding a coherent system of ideas that allows house-room to hypnotic effects, hysterical paralyses, and hypochondria. Here the link between (unconscious) thought and emotion, on one hand, and (partly) physical manifestations like paralysis, on the other, is not simply causal. There is a link of meaning; one might say that the paralysis is one way, or perhaps the only way, the subject has at that time of expressing unconscious feeling. It is the psychic representation of the body that is involved in the symptom, not so much the neural and physical body.

To give a brief example. I have reason to believe that X's apparently inexplicable onset of an inability to play right handed at tennis, golf and other sports is an inhibition whose meaning is related to his unconscious fear of using this hand to kill someone. Just before the quasi-paralysis began in X his older brother had been convicted of murdering a man with a knife. X was very close to this brother and greatly admired him. I am ready to accept, without unease or fear of incoherence, the explanation of the paralysis along such lines. Here his phantasy ('I might kill my opponent but I must not') is at work through and expressed in the paralysis.

Where my unease tends to emerge is in relation to psychosomatic conditions, in which, as in natural expressions of emotion, there *are* obvious chemical changes. The person with irritable bowel syndrome really does have changes in his gut, which operate at the cell level, at the enzymal level, and at the perceptual level. Sometimes I feel troubled by the question: how can unconscious or conscious mental events alter one's physiology in such permanent syndromes? And how can we *ever* know (philosophical, epistemological question) that these actual illnesses have psychological determinants?

For the most part, I am not prevented from thinking analytically in these areas. An example. A patient Y who is liable to the bowel syndrome is afflicted by phobias. When the phobia becomes intense, or when he is phobic about the possibility of intense phobic states, his syndrome recurs. He feels horrible cramps in his stomach, and is likely to have diarrhoea. I believe that this has to do with a compulsive wish to evacuate everything from inside him. The wish does not take the form of, say, a dream of evacuation, as with another patient (in four times weekly analysis) who dreamed of putting four bags of rubbish outside the door of his house. Nor does he dream of internal conflict or war; Y actually has to go to the toilet. Later in the analysis, Y developed constipation, which alternated with the by now less prolonged episodes of diarrhoea. At this later time, we were able to see that there was a more complex psychological process. He wished to dump his bad stuff into another person, but this presented him with a double fear: would he damage the other as a result? And would he lose things of value to himself? So the spasm of pain seemed to express precisely the ambivalent anxiety that he felt psychologically. Either way – whether he let loose, or whether he was blocked up – he was exposed to extremely critical internal voices, one saying 'So you think you're so caring!' and the other 'So you think you're brave!'

In a second case (in which the therapist was in supervision with me), the power of the projective identification into the body had a surprising further effect. This patient suffered from distressing irritated bowel syndrome. She did not turn up for her last session before a long break. There was no telephone message. Half way through the session time, the therapist – who had gone through a range of feelings from worry and concern to frustration and anger – suddenly herself had a bout of violent diarrhoea. Since this was not a general problem of hers, and she felt no further discomfort subsequently, it seemed likely that she was the recipient of a powerful projective process from the patient.

Patients who are functioning at the level of these patients are bound to find insightful interpretations hard to make use of. Their level of functioning is concrete; that is, there is little or no room for symbolisation of the wish to evacuate a horrible feeling/thought from the mind.

At times, however, despite my belief that such interpretations are on the right lines, I can become radically uncertain. I can feel paralysed; or bereft of all belief, like a religious person in a crisis of faith. In less out-of-touch moments I understand such help-lessness as the outcome partly of projections from my patients, partly of my own intolerance of any delay in perfect understanding, and partly a result of my confusion about body and mind. My omnipotence is at work, interfering with the healthy struggle towards truth. I thus arrogantly spit out or negate hope. I have turned difficulty into impossibility. If I ask myself why I am liable to such reactions to these conditions but not to 'natural expressions of emotion', I think I might first note the former conditions' persistence over time, whereas the latter are relatively short-lived. Moreover, from what I regard as a proper psychoanalytic point of view, I see the psychosomatic conditions as organised defences, which have a life of their own in the body. As the brief example of Y suggests, they may, at least sometimes, be seen as expressions of primitive object relations with limited symbolic elaboration.

4. Can psychoanalysis throw light on the body-mind nexus?

What I hope to show is that there are two movements in psycho-analytic thinking in this area. The first is that, when unconscious psychological affects take the form of physical symptoms we aim to reclaim (or 'claim') the psychological from the somatic. We slowly arrive at attempts to understand the meaning of such symptoms and their formation. And we sometimes find that if these are emotionally accepted by the patient, there will be shifts in the level of functioning towards a fuller emotional life, and subsequently less need for the merely bodily symptoms and reports. The aim of the analytic work is to help our patients to own or re-own that which been projected into the body, usually as a result of the fact that certain feelings have been unbearable and unthinkable. Thus we aim to bring into the field of thought, into the mind, that which has been ejected from the mind and expressed in and through the body.

The second, and related, tendency is to make use of a model which acknowledges the way our sense of ourselves begins with, and is rooted in our emerging sense of ourselves as encased by skin, as existing in and through our bodies. 'The first Ego is a Body Ego'. And again: 'The idea is that there is a proto-mental level at which . . . emotional elements are undifferentiated from physical ones' (Meltzer, pp. 9–10). At the raw, primitive level, we are absolutist, concrete and ruthless. The capacity for symbol-making is limited. A brief example of a colleague's: A patient is told that there will be no session next day, and says, in panic, 'My arm has gone. Something went.' This suggests that he experienced the other not as fully other, whose prospective absence could be experienced as painful, but as part of himself, in a concrete bodily way. There was simply concrete loss of a part of himself. Another brief example. A very young child vomits when her parents leave her with someone else. We might understand this as her throwing up, out, the bad feelings she experiences inside herself. A few months later, the same child allows parents to go out, but requires a ritualised 'good-bye' and a small material token from each parent, and which stands for the parents. Later still she can tolerate the separation without somatisation, and without material tokens or symbols. She can expect that they will return, trust them to remember her, and hold them in mind herself (see Bion 1962: 34, section 9). Psychoanalysis expands the meaning of what may start by being thought of in a restricted physical sense. (Incidentally, the concept of sexuality is one such example.)

I suggest that if we can grasp both these aspects of mind and body we may be less tempted to fall into, or slide towards, Cartesian dualism. Then we will be less compelled to ask the question 'how can we understand the connection between mind and body?' but will be more likely to ask rather, 'how can we understand the developmental moves from body-mind to mind and the anti-developmental moves in the opposite direction?' We may also come to understand also how inevitable it is that we are all liable to fall back to earlier ways of functioning when we become anxious.

5. Anzieu's concept of a skin ego

At this point I want to give you an idea of the lines of thought that I am advocating by briefly describing the work of the French psychoanalyst, Didier Anzieu. He offers an account of the mind and its development that fully takes on board, through myth and phantasy, this evolution from sensorial or physical modes of experience.

Anzieu presents a notion of skin ego, in his book of the same name. The skin ego has its own evolution. There is an early stage at which the baby feels it shares a common skin with the object, which forms the plane or axis with mother and self symmetrically placed around it. I find this useful as a way of thinking about expectations we all have to some degree at some times, of being instantaneously understood by our lovers or analysts. The skin can also be a map of the mental terrain, as happens naturally in cases of blushing, sexual arousal, and some forms of pallor. In certain states it is the only map available for the subject as for the other.

The next stage requires the suppression of this common skin, and the recognition of the fact that each has his or her own skin, a process which involves resistance and pain. According to him, then, the skin ego underlies the possibility of thought and of the emerging psychic ego. I find that in my work images of the skin, as well as some forms of skin problem, can be expressions of powerful psychic states.

6. Personal example of struggle to move from somatic to psychological level

I will now offer a personal example of the struggle to move from one level to the other.

Feeling anxious about the task of writing this paper, and of having something interesting to say to you, I can't sleep. Half-formed thoughts career around my mind. In retrospect, I might describe my state as a mixture of fear and excitement. In the middle of the night I feel more than usually perplexed about body and mind questions, and the hopelessness of any possible solution. In the middle of this confusion, I get cramp in my calves and feet. I have to jump out of bed, and arch and press my feet to the ground. Here I am, with a somatic symptom of the very process that I am intellectually stuck in, the kind of intellectual

cramp Wittgenstein refers to. The wretched body won't stay out
of the picture. These cramps are, without doubt, physiological
events. There are presumably changes in the chemistry of the
muscles. Drinking water might help, or taking salt pills. They
might be treatable by a medical doctor. Yet I believe that such an
explanation, and possible cure, is only part of the truth. I have
a sense that my cramp results from my tension about writing the
paper. How am I to account for it?

I am not able – or willing – to give a full account of all the
emotions that enter into such nocturnal states, or keep me from
sleeping. I am aware that by offering you this small item of
personal history and my own thoughts on it I lay myself open
not only to your supervision but to your interpretations. I am
aware too of how likely I am to be prone to self-deception or
over-confidence in my mini-self-analysis. However, one reason
for including this is to underline my claim that psychosomatic
tendencies exist in us all. Another is that in a public lecture
issues of confidentiality are problematical.

So I will say something. I know myself well enough to suspect
that when I feel inept, or incompetent, in anticipation of giving
a paper, this kind of anxiety is often an attempt at a solution to
a personal problem. The problem is that 'behind' the felt, and
sometimes enacted, incompetence is a phantasy of omnipotence. According to this other part of me, my ego-ideal, I should
be giving the definitive answer to the mind-body problem that
has led philosophers and others to such counter-intuitive and
implausible answers. I must, at one fell swoop, clear up all the
confusions and falsehoods not only in psychoanalysis but in
philosophy too. However, I also know that this is, to say the least,
a tall order, so, rather than be seen, by myself or others, as arro-
gant or grandiose, I make myself more stupid than I actually am.
The cramps represent, I think, this uncomfortable and conflict-
ual self-restriction.

What's more, these painful psycho-physical events could
represent the punishment of the cruel superego, which regards
my self-importance with self-righteous scorn. Shakespeare was
psychologically right when he talked about the cramps that
Prospero causes Caliban; the base side of ourselves is constantly
being pinched, cramped, inhibited by the mind's magic-working
despot.

Another idea of Wittgenstein's is useful here: a picture holds
me captive. I am held in painful inner chains by my warring

pictures or phantasies of myself. One picture is that I can offer the best ever answer to the thorny and perpetual problems of free will and the mind/body problems; the other that such pride needs to be curbed, and deserves punishment and persecution.

As I began, in the night in question, to calm down through thinking along these lines, I fell asleep. I woke at my usual time, having had a dream. *I am captain of the England cricket team. England are batting, facing a small target. We have not lost a wicket. Geoff Boycott is struggling. His partner, who is a left handed batsman, has recently been in good form. There is a mix-up between the batsmen, and instead of completing an easy single, the left hander is run out. Boycott seems to be responsible. I am outraged with him, and have the thought: 'he must never again be picked for this team'. But I then think, still in the dream, firstly, that, far from scoring slowly, he has in fact scored most of the runs so far in this innings. And secondly, I wonder what he had to suffer in the way of learning in a hard school, of being put down, and run out when he was a boy?*

On waking I try to think about the dream. I can't link it with any particular event of the previous day. I wonder if the two batsmen represent part-selves, and if the dream says that I am running out, that is dismissing, excluding, another part of my inner team, of myself, the less orthodox, left-handed part of myself. Then my subsequent outrage against Boycott may be understood as self-hatred. But I go on, still dreaming, to moderate this pejorative view ('Boycott' wasn't so bad). Then it is possible for me to tolerate and forgive this selfish part of me, this 'player' in the team that constitutes myself, faults and all. It seems that this other part of me which comments and thinks within the dream can allow that I/Boycott am selfish but that this has antecedents, and has not prevented me from scoring runs, even, perhaps, being capable of producing ideas in the present 'innings', the task of writing this paper. (No doubt there are other many elements in the dream, including ambivalence towards the left-hander – running him out – and the aggressive aspects of legs and feet like kicking and treading on. This is not meant to be an exhaustive analysis of the dream.)

As I thought about the dream later, I concluded that it was only after my period of reflection in the night that I was able to have the dream that actually gives a fuller meaning to the cramps. Previously, I had been unable to represent my situation psychically, in a dream. Rather, at the beginning I simply had this painful feeling in the body, itself both a cramping of thought and feeling, and, as the dream suggests, potentially a representation of my refusing to run, to exchange views productively with the side of me that is identified with the despised body. Thus by means of my reflections and then the dream I had reclaimed part of my psyche that had been temporarily lost. I found a means to move myself from the merely physiological to a more representational, symbolic way of experiencing.

I have to acknowledge the fact that this growth in my capacity to evolve a fully emotional awareness, to generate a psychic register for what had been experienced as bodily, was an achievement. To generalise, for each human being it is a development worthy of amazement and pride were it not that we all, more or less, manage it, with a great deal of help, in our first years of life. This development is the work of chiselling out a mind from a matrix of body-mind. For whatever account we give of the earliest psychological states of the infant, we all agree that there is a struggle, which is in fact life-long, to develop fuller mind-body discriminations. My small-scale reclamation of mindfulness, mind-full-ness, presence of mind, is presumably a repetition of the initial chiselling out; we need a concept of 'clamation'.

7. Postscript

Throughout this paper you may have noticed a hint of an undeveloped shadow to its substance. As a matter of fact the paper has evolved from an earlier attempt in which the central aim was to suggest that these psychoanalytic theories might have an impact on philosophical ideas of the body mind problem.

I think now that that earlier project was probably over-ambitious. However I am interested in these questions. And in a preliminary way I will make a few, more modest, points.

First one finds in clinical practice neurotic versions of philosophical doubts and theories, as Wisdom and Wittgenstein showed. A paranoid patient feels he is stuck in his own world, and complains that he can never know whether anyone else loves him or hates him. One might compare the philosopher who says we can never know the mind of another. Another patient worries obsessively, unable ever to feel confident that he is safe from error; he is like a philosopher who worries endlessly about the possibility of knowing anything. A third patient sneers at those who worry themselves about moral issues or who hope for love:

they are in his mind pathetic creatures; whenever his conscience begins to trouble him, he becomes a sceptic about moral questions, like the 'So What?' school of ethics from the 1930s. Behaviourism is paralleled by the patient who can only infer his own inner life from his own behaviour, or who reduces need to materialistic desires. More relevantly to this paper, the analyst's neurotic doubts about body and mind interpenetrations echoes the Cartesian philosophy's scepticism and its implausible solutions (such as that the answer lies in a special gland linking brain and mind, or in the epiphenomenalism according to which psychic events are merely the shadows cast by brain activity). My quasi-philosophical cramps relate more to this Cartesian issue, and my sense of something mysterious about how mind can affect the body. We need to remind ourselves occasionally of the ways in which the mind and the body are inextricably involved, as in natural expressions of emotion and anxiety.

Secondly, in my oscillation as a psychoanalyst between grandiosity and impotence, tendencies towards omniscience and utter ignorance, there are also analogies with philosophy and its anxiety about knowledge in general. In their own ways philosophical 'solutions' reflect such oscillations. Philosophical assertions of special ways of knowing the field which is in dispute are akin to grandiosity. A key work is 'intuit', as in G.E. Moore's account of ethical knowledge. We just know, without having to make any difficult inferences from verifiable facts of description. Such a potent position can alternate restlessly with its impotent relative, scepticism, and its neighbour, reductionism.

Thirdly, philosophy is much clearer about the nature of its doubts than psychoanalysis. As Wittgenstein said, the man who doubts the existence of the external world does not doubt that under his trousers he wears pants. To give another example, the Idealist philosopher Bradley was reported to have ended one lecture with the following words: 'In this lecture I have proved that Space does not exist. In next week's lecture I will show that Time does not exist. Next week's lecture will be in room 6 at 10 o'clock.' Philosophers are not, that is, deluded, and their doubts are not really about the actual contents of the world, whereas my doubts as a psychoanalyst are at times a confused mixture of practical doubts and conceptual ones, and patients can be deluded.

Fourthly, the occurrence of my cramps in these border areas of psychoanalysis and philosophy remind me powerfully of those I was prone to when doing philosophy. When I showed a friend, someone who like me had previously studied philosophy, an earlier version of this paper, he wrote: 'I had a set of reactions that somehow illustrated parts of what I think you are saying. I found myself experiencing an intense set of memories, the kind of memories that can come when listening to a piece of music. I felt what it used to be like doing philosophy – which, for me, was unlike any other kind of intellectual effort. I "saw" the library where I often worked, and "smelt" its smells, and even "heard" the murmuring sounds that go on around one in such places. More strikingly, I felt strong physical sensations that I always had when puzzling over the big philosophical ideas – a turning in the stomach, a slight shivering of excitement, something a bit like vertigo, sudden collapses into episodes of panic and despair. I think these are feelings that you refer to – linked to Wittgenstein's "cramp", but more to that feeling you identify of having a sense of needing to solve, and the excitement of thinking you are able to solve, at last, some huge and cosmic issue; and then the reactive sense of having no hope of being able to do so, and therefore a feeling – also in the body – of being stupid and stuck. And, in my case, a strange lurching back and forth between these states of mind and body – with the lurching itself having somatic forms'. I present this to show that I am not alone!

Finally, following Wisdom and Wittgenstein, I wish to note some similarities in the treatment of philosophical and psychological confusions, lurchings. In both there is an effort to lay bare the 'picture' (Wittgenstein) 'that holds us captive', the unconscious phantasy that we cannot own consciously. In each there is an attempt to allow the subject (patient or philosopher) to discover and reclaim the 'unthought known' (Bollas). In the case of philosophy the stress is on aspects of what is available to everyone (it is not arcane or requiring research, nor is it treated as uniquely personal), and on that which leads to confusion when one attempts to related one category of thought to another. Philosophy of body/mind, for instance, deals with confusions and problems within the everyday concepts covered by these terms, which usually cause little pragmatic trouble, but which can give rise to paradoxical theories about what must be the case. In psychoanalysis, the stress is more on aspects of what is privately disowned, or unthought, in the present and past of the patient.

8. Conclusion

When we cannot contain in the skin of our minds whatever disturbs and affects us, this disturbance is likely to be experienced in our bodies, in ways that may change our physiology. One way in which primitive states of emotion are naturally expressed is through our bodies.

Bion and Anzieu have given us a model which helps us to understand how we create and discover mind and self out of a more confused state of body/mind, and out of a self/other amalgam. As we progress emotionally, and can bear anxiety, guilt, and extremes of feelings with the help of symbolisation, we gradually modify them, and are less stuck in rigid, damaging and meaningless 'solutions'. My experience tends to confirm the idea that our body has from the start entered in to the growth of the sense of self as an autonomous and integrated being in world, and that the body self, the skin self, remain core elements in ourselves. When these achievements have been for whatever reasons, insubstantial, the person lacks, in layers of himself, capacities to register events through the symbolisation of thinking.

But as I have argued, the achievements of a psychic skin, and of the capacity to bear separateness and separation, are always partial. Wisdom is also a matter of having the humility to hold on to the fact that the primitive is with us throughout our lives. No man is an island, entire of itself: similarly no mind is mind, entire unto itself, and separated like an island from the body. Human bodies cannot be reduced to mere collections of chemicals. Mind permeates our bodies, and vice versa.[1]

References

Aisenstein, M. (1993). 'Psychosomatic Solution or Somatic Outcome', in *International Journal of Psychoanalysis*, vol. 74, pp. 371–380.

[1] I am grateful to many people for their help in the writing of this paper, including particularly Sally Weintrobe, Neville Symington, Evanthe Blandy, Nicola Abel-Hirsch, Margot Waddell, and Hugh Brody.

In this paper I do not attempt to give an account of anything like the whole range of somatic expressions. I limit myself to those psychosomatic symptoms which appear to 'represent' or point to the states of mind that inform them. I do not address illnesses acquired and retained for secondary gain, nor the many ways in which an individual's particular area of physical vulnerability is made use of in states of psychological stress. Nor again do I discuss ways in which the person's vitality is expressed in bodily ways.

Anzieu, D. (1989). *The Skin Ego* (Newhaven and London: Yale University Press).

Bion, W. (1961). *Experiences in Groups* (London: Tavistock).

Bion, W. (1962). *Learning from Experience.* (London: Tavistock).

Bollas, C. (1987). *The Shadow of the Object: Psychoanalysis of the Unthought Known.* (London: Free Associations).

Bradley, FH. [1893] (1925). *Appearance and Reality* (London: George Allen & Unwin Ltd.).

Descartes, R. [1641] (1967). *The Meditations,* in *The Philosophical Works of Descartes* (Cambridge: University Press).

Freud, S. [1923] (1961). *The Ego and the Id* (London: Hogarth).

Leibniz, G. [1714] (1898). *The Monadology,* in *The Monadology and Other Writings* (Oxford: University Press).

McDougall, J. (1989). *Theatres of the Body* (New York: Norton).

Meltzer, D. (1978). *The Kleinian Development,* vol. 3 (Strathclyde: Clunie).

Shakespeare, W. [1611] (1978). *The Tempest,* in *Complete Works* (Oxford: University Press).

Wisdom, J. (1953). *Philosophy and Psychoanalysis* (Oxford: Blackwell).

Wittgenstein, L. (1953). *Philosophical Investigations* (Oxford: Blackwell).

INDEX

CPSIA information can be obtained at www.ICGtesting.com
Printed in the USA
LVOW11s0351221113

362353LV00012B/154/A